Literature's Silent Language: Nonverbal Communication

American University Studies

Series IV
English Language and Literature

Vol. 19

PETER LANG
New York · Berne · Frankfurt am Main

Stephen R. Portch

Literature's Silent Language

Nonverbal Communication

PETER LANG
New York · Berne · Frankfurt am Main

Library of Congress Cataloging in Publication Data

Portch, Stephen R.
Literature's Silent Language.

(American University Studies. Series IV, English
Language and Literature; vol. 19)
Bibliography: p.
Includes index.
1. Short stories, American – History and criticism.
2. Nonverbal communication in literature.   3. Characters
and characteristics in literature.   4. Fiction –
Technique.   I. Title.   II. Series.
PS374.N65P67   1985   813'.01'09   84-48083
ISBN 0-8204-0172-2
ISSN 0741-0700

CIP-Kurztitelaufnahme der Deutschen Bibliothek

Portch, Stephen R.:
Literature's Silent Language: Nonverbal
Communication / Stephen R. Portch. – New York;
Berne; Frankfurt am Main: Lang, 1985.
(American University Studies: Ser. 4,
English Language and Literature; Vol. 19)
ISBN 0-8204-0172-2

NE: American University Studies / 04

© Peter Lang Publishing, Inc., New York 1985

Printed by Lang Druck, Inc., Liebefeld/Berne (Switzerland)

TABLE OF CONTENTS

ACKNOWLEDGMENTS

I wish to thank those who have made this book possible. Professor Robert N. Hudspeth of the Pennsylvania State University English department provided the spark for the topic, the challenge of a scholar, and the encouragement of a friend. His colleagues Professors Philip Young, James M. Rambeau, and William Toombs strengthened the original draft with their close readings and constructive comments.

The University of Wisconsin Marathon Center Foundation Inc., through the UWMC Research and Professional Development Committee, generously provided me with a summer grant to assist with the research and manuscript preparation costs. Many of the faculty, administration, and staff of the UW Centers gave me financial, or practical, or moral support. My students and community audiences helped me focus my ideas on this topic. Vicki Allaback, June Roloff, and Sally Paul gave me typing assistance. Ann Brooks prepared the final copy; Jennifer Thiel assisted with the proof-reading.

Candy Stover—a fine critic, editor, and writer—generously read and incisively commented on early drafts. Henry and Carol Sams offered me invaluable encouragement, advice, and assistance in the early days of my career.

Barbara, my wife, helped me by cutting and pasting drafts (while wishing someone would invent a word-processor) and tolerating the hours of silent seclusion. My parents, Graham and Thelma Portch, and my in-laws, Alan and Helen Barrows, supported me in establishing an academic career.

vi

A book of this kind depends heavily on examples from literature. For permission to reprint longer quotations, I wish to recognize and thank the following:

I also appreciate those publishers who interpreted my quotation as "fair use"; full sources are given in both the notes and selected bibliography.

To use much modified versions of two earlier articles on the topic, I thank *The Hemingway Review* ("The Hemingway Touch," Fall 1982, 43-48) and *The Journal of General Education* ("Writing Without Words: A Nonverbal Approach to Reading Fiction," Spring 1982, 84-101) and their editors (Charles M. Oliver and Caroline D. and Robert B. Eckhardt, respectively) for the early confidence they showed in my work in this area.

Without the encouragement, cooperation, and support of the above, this book would not have been possible. Their contributions are gratefully acknowledged.

Chapter 1
INTRODUCTION

Fie, fie upon her!
There's language in her eyes, her cheek, her lip.
Nay, her foot speaks; her wanton spirits look out
At every joint and motive of her body.

> Ulysses in William Shakespeare's
> *Troilus and Cressida*, IV. 5.54-57.

Shakespeare was on to something. The body oozes messages constantly and communication occurs both consciously and unconsciously, both verbally and nonverbally. The study of the nonverbal aspects of communication has attracted, among others, psychologists and psychiatrists, sociologists and anthropologists, ethologists and linguists. It has spawned a vocabulary of its own ranging from "kinesics" to "pupillometrics," from "paralanguage" to "proxemics," from "haptics" to "chronemics." But the systematic application of nonverbal theory to the reading of literature has been largely ignored. Readers frequently listen carefully to what characters say but glide through descriptions of what characters do. This bothered Henry James.

In his essay "The Art of Fiction," James reveals his awareness that the nonverbal can indeed trigger communication in alert and perceptive readers: "When the mind is imaginative . . . it converts the very pulses of the air into revelations."[1] He refers to the importance of fiction attempting "to represent life" in all its shades and to reaching beyond the artificial boundaries of character, plot, and description; the writer must have "the power to guess the unseen from the seen, to trace the implication of things, to judge the whole piece by the pattern."[2] And the pattern of life for James included the nonverbal: "It is an incident for a woman to stand up with her hand resting on a table and look at you in a certain way. . . . At the same time it is an expression of character."[3]

Clearly, much of the interpretation of characters in literature and people in real life--their motives, drives, relationships with people and to situations--depends on understanding and revealing their emotional states. Dialogue provides one aspect for examination and subsequent interpretation. Conscious action provides another. But perhaps the most potent, and least understood, element is nonverbal communication. One way to add to our understanding is to distinguish between verbal and nonverbal communication. For instance, although the capability to use language is innate, the performance of language--its vocabulary, sounds, and rules--must be learned.

The capacity for nonverbal communication is also innate, but a considerable controversy exists over the degree to which the actual performance is learned. Ethologists support the evolutionary, behaviorists the environmental. The former suggests that nonverbal signs have evolved based on survival value and marshal evidence of similarities in nonverbal signs across cultures. The latter suggest that nonverbal signs have been learned through cultural lessons and marshal evidence of differences in nonverbal signs across cultures. Paul Ekman, Wallace V. Friesen, and John Bear identify three types of conscious nonverbal signs: "popular," "unique," and "multi-meaning." The "popular" has the same meaning in several cultures, such as the headshake for "no." The "unique" is a sign specific to only one culture. The "multi-meaning" has one meaning in one culture, a different meaning in another. The last is the most dangerous. Take, for example, the "A-okay" gesture, made with the thumb and forefinger. In America, it is a positive gesture, but it "has an insulting meaning in France and Belgium: 'You're worth zero.' In parts of Southern Italy it means 'asshole,' while in

Greece and Turkey it is a vulgar sexual invitation."[4] Maybe phrase books need

to be expanded to include nonverbal signs.

Differences also exist in the structure and in the capacity of the two

types of communication. The nonverbal does not appear to be as complex or as

versatile as the verbal. Efforts have been made to identify the equivalents

of phonemes and syntactical rules but with only limited success. Furthermore,

the nonverbal lacks the capabilities of reflexiveness, of indicating tense,

and of referencing the negative. The verbal can talk about itself; the

nonverbal can rarely comment on itself. The verbal can indicate present,

past, or future; the nonverbal can only clearly indicate the present. The

verbal can testify to the absence of something; the nonverbal cannot directly

indicate absence. To Kenneth Burke, this last point is critical: "The

essential distinction between the verbal and the nonverbal is the fact that

language adds the peculiar possibility of the negative."[5]

The gap between the verbal and nonverbal does not even narrow at the

center of communication: the message. As Judee K. Burgoon and Thomas Saine in

The Unspoken Dialogue: An Introduction to Nonverbal Communication suggest,

"Nonverbal messages are generally more powerful than verbal ones."[6] For

example, they point out that the nonverbal message, whatever its intended

purpose, invariably reveals emotions. Further, the nonverbal has far greater

potential for conveying multiple messages simultaneously and for having those

messages received directly through sensory stimulation rather than filtering

through the thought process. Finally, Burgoon and Saine suggest that although

the nonverbal may occasionally be manipulated to deceive, most people receive

and perceive nonverbal messages as spontaneous and, therefore, as more likely

to be honest.

The implications of these message characteristics for the interpretation

of literature are manifold. T.S. Eliot suggested in his essay on "Hamlet and

His Problems," that neither dialogue nor action exists in a void; for Eliot, the true key to unlocking the emotional lives of characters turns on the ability to perceive the relationship of seemingly disparate messages:

> The only way of expressing emotion in the form of art is by finding an "objective correlative"; in other words, a set of objects, a situation, a chain of events which shall be the formula of that particular emotion; such that when the external facts, which must terminate in sensory experience, are given, the emotion is immediately evoked.[7]

Although Eliot wrote before the wide interest in the nonverbal had developed, he focuses on the relationship between unspoken language and both the context and the spoken as a method of successfully presenting emotion in art.

Further, Eliot touches on another aspect of the effectiveness of the nonverbal emphasized by later nonverbalists: its ability to stimulate a sensory response. In real life, the nonverbal seems to have the potential to by-pass thought routes. In literature (with the exception of performed drama), this would not seem to be possible since the written words have to be absorbed by the eyes and consumed by the mind. But both Eliot and Ernest Hemingway (the writer, Hemingway said, can control readers' responses to make them "feel something more than they understood"[8]) suggest that perhaps not all that readers receive from literature follows conscious paths, that possibly readers create their own fictional images as they read—images which they unconsciously react to with their senses to receive the basic messages.

Also, in real life, several nonverbal messages can be sent simultaneously. Again, in literature, this would not seem to be possible since the written word has the same chronological limitation as the spoken word: only one word can be spoken at a time. But an approximation is possible. For example, an author can choose to describe a number of nonverbal activities by a character before (or between) dialogue--activities which, when examined together, communicate multiple messages.

The most important element in Burgoon and Saine's characteristics of nonverbal messages for literary interpretation is the basic truthfulness of such messages. We lie better with words than with the nonverbal; in fact, the nonverbal frequently contradicts the verbal. A character in fiction may speak deceptively while giving clues to this deception through various described body movements. And a character may even reflect more truthfulness through one part of the body than another. Readers who miss what Ekman and Friesen term "Nonverbal Leakage and Clues to Deception"[9] in a character may miss the point of a story.

Certain authors make considerable use of the nonverbal to contradict the verbal. J. D. Salinger, for example, seems particularly conscious of this technique. His memorable character Esme in "For Esme--with Love and Squalor" emits confidence and precociousness verbally, yet she betrays her insecurity and nervousness nonverbally. At age thirteen, Esme approaches a foreign soldier and, rather formulaically, embarks on an almost flawless (she has trouble with the words "intrinsically" and "prolific") exhibition of verbal ("gregarious," "extrovert," "superficial," "posterity," "extenuating") and social maturity. But her hands and feet reveal her mental and personal distress. She bit "reflectively at the cuticle of her thumb"[10] and "almost instantly, closed her hands--her nails were bitten down to the quick."[11] She shakes hands with "a nervous hand, damp at the palm."[12] Her legs aren't much steadier. Twice "she crossed one foot over the other and, looking down, aligned the toes of her shoes."[13]

Interestingly, Salinger uses hands and feet rather than the face to reveal the basic contradiction; his choices exactly parallel what the experiments of Ekman and Friesen support: that although literally harder to hide, we learn to control, to inhibit, and to dissimulate our faces but not our hands and feet. Stephen Crane also seems intuitively to have been aware of this. In *Maggie: A Girl of the Streets*, the desperate Maggie decides to approach a man who with "his beaming, chubby face was a picture of benevolence and kind-heartedness. His eyes shone good will." But no sooner does she approach him than "he made a convulsive movement and saved his respectability by a vigorous side-step."[14] So although the nonverbal can generally be trusted more than the verbal, some components of the nonverbal--such as the hands and feet--are more reliable indicators of truth than others.

The context of communication is clearly critical. Words, for instance, carry the charge of the speaker, the spark of the situation. The words themselves are symbols; they become symbols of symbols when written; and the context adds further to the symbolism. The same is true of unspoken dialogue: context communicates. Those who have ignored context in their sexily-titled books on body language have done the study of nonverbal communication considerable harm. Such authors turn a complex communication system into simple equations, wherein certain body signals have consistent meanings.

Edward T. Hall does not make that mistake. Indeed, he recognizes that our very understanding of mankind depends on communication and context:

> What is characteristically man--in fact, what gives man his identity no matter where he is born--is his culture, the total communication framework: words, actions, postures, gestures, tones of voice, facial expressions, the way he handles time, space, and materials, and the way he works, plays, makes love, and defends himself. All these things and more are complete communication systems with meanings that can be read correctly only if one is familiar with the behavior in its historical, social, and cultural context.[15]

In defining mankind, Hall comes close to a comprehensive definition of nonverbal communication.

A widely accepted definition seems elusive. Perhaps the most eloquent but barest definition comes from Edward Sapir: nonverbal communication is "an elaborate and secret code that is written nowhere, known by none, and understood by all."[16] Almost every other author on the nonverbal attempts a definition, too, but without any clear consensus. Maybe Albert Mehrabian has the solution; he prefers "the concept of implicit communication . . . to the misnomer, nonverbal communication"[17]--but his courage seems to have failed him when it came to the title of his book: *Nonverbal Communication*. Although a neat and convenient definition has yet to surface, Randall P. Harrison warns that unless we want to drown in the depths of confusion, the floodgates of definition must be closed:

> The term nonverbal communication has been applied to a broad range of phenomena: everything from facial expression and gesture to fashion and status symbol, from dance and drama to music and mime, from flow of affect to flow of traffic, from the territoriality of animals to the protocol of diplomats, from extra-sensory perception to analog computers, from the rhetoric of violence to the rhetoric of topless dancers.[18]

Classification offers no easy solutions, either. A review of the classification systems reveals them to be nearly as topless as the definitions--albeit nowhere near as naked. Some systems include up to eighteen items. But two systems seem to offer useful divisions, some of which can be fruitfully applied to literary interpretation. Ekman and Friesen classify five types of nonverbal signs according to their functions, and Burgoon and Saine identify seven nonverbal codes.[19]

The former system has a narrow focus, placing a spotlight on the behavior of people. This approach views nonverbal communication as a series of physical signs given by one person and possibly received by others. The latter system has a much broader scope, spreading a floodlight across all the elements over which people have some control. This approach views nonverbal communication as multi-dimensional, including not only direct physical elements (such as tone of voice), but also indirect yet humanly controllable elements (such as use of time or choice of clothing). Both systems include a range of behavior from the conscious to the unconscious; both systems acknowledge that the degree of accuracy with which the signs will be read and the codes will be decoded varies with the sensitivity of the receivers. Together these two systems provide a comprehensive method of separating and recognizing nonverbal communication.

The Ekman and Friesen classification uses five basic terms: (1) emblems, (2) illustrators, (3) regulators, (4) affect displays (renamed "body clues" in this book) and (5) adaptors (or body manipulators).

(1) Emblems are intentional, explicit gestures which substitute for the verbal--usually when that channel is physically blocked. The hitchhiker's thumb and the umpire's signals; the bending beckoning finger and the sudden obscene gesture--all are emblems. Many, like the last, differ between cultures, but all are sent consciously with the specific intent to communicate.

(2) Illustrators accompany and augment the verbal message. When we speak, we frequently illustrate our points--perhaps with a pounded fist or pointed finger; perhaps with the drawing of an aerial picture or with the signifying of distance; perhaps with the rhythm of a conductor or with the flair of an actor. Like emblems, illustrators are primarily conscious if not quite as explicit. Unlike emblems, they usually occur simultaneously with the spoken. These first two categories clarify the most overused and misapplied

of all nonverbal terms: gesture. Emblems and illustrators are gestures: that is, primarily conscious messages.

(3) Regulators help control verbal interaction. As Michael Argyle shows, regulators have a number of punctuation functions: a shift of gaze can provide a pause; a raised eyebrow or upward head movement can signal a question.[20] Most importantly, though, regulators involve both speaker and listener(s). In our culture speakers can receive reinforcement from listeners if, for example, listeners nod their heads periodically. The length of a speech can be controlled by regulators in what Argyle calls the synchronization of utterances; he reviews experiments which catalog ways a listener can take the floor or decline an offer of the floor and a speaker can keep the floor or offer to yield the floor. Furthermore, the regulators can control more than just who speaks: "They tell the speakers to continue, repeat, elaborate, hurry up, become more interesting, less salacious. . . . They can tell the listener to pay special attention, to wait just a minute more,"[21] and so on. Like emblems and illustrators, regulators have specific differences among cultures. Unlike emblems and illustrators, regulation occurs with little consciousness on the part of the regulator. Authors occasionally use regulators in dialogue. Flannery O'Connor, for example, in "Good Country People," has Mrs. Hopewell attempt to regulate her conversation with a Bible salesman when he starts to talk about God: "She stood up."[22]

(4) Body clues indicate emotion either intentionally or unintentionally. Ekman and Friesen concentrate primarily on facial displays of emotion, but other parts of the body (for example, hands, feet, and overall posture) also reveal emotional states. Ekman points out that typically displays of emotion are quick both in onset and duration. Certain emotions, Ekman feels, trigger natural, evolutionary, and universal facial signs: happiness, fear, anger, surprise, sadness, and disgust. And although most of the time people reveal their emotions involuntarily, sometimes they can

deceive with their faces--as did Salinger's Esme and Crane's character. Furthermore, difficulties arise in the interpretation of body clues not just because they are usually fleeting, or so numberous (Ekman and Friesen's "The Facial Action System" identified more than 10,000 distinct facial actions), or reveal a blend of emotions, but also because people differ in their ability to spot and interpret facial displays of emotion.

(5) Adaptors originated for practical purposes and have become assimilated into behavioral patterns. For example, the clenching of a fist in anger has the practical purpose of preparing the hand to administer a blow. But more often than not, the fist is clenched to signal anger without a blow being struck. Ekman modified and added to the original concept of adaptors by identifying a concept termed "body manipulators," which "are movements in which one part of the body does something to another part."[23] He included both the use of body actions (for example, licking the lips) and the use of props for a noninstrumental purpose (for example, striking a match is not a body manipulator, but fiddling with the match is). A person using body manipulators has little consciousness of the acts. An observer, however, can realize information from the body manipulators--even though there's been no intent to communicate. This is general information (such as say, nervousness) rather than very specific emotions. Robin's anxiety for instance, in Nathaniel Hawthorne's "My Kinsman, Major Molineux" can, in part, be detected from his manipulating his oak cudgel as much as his using it.

Three of the five components in the original Ekman and Friesen classification communicate implicitly: regulators, body clues, and adaptors. Since literature (except for the most didactic) also communicates implicitly, these three elements would seem to have particular value for literary interpretation. An awareness of what regulators, body clues, and adaptors may imply about a character and inter-relationships can add a considerable dimension to the interpretation of literature. That is not to say, though, that authors do not allow their characters to use emblems and illustrators. They do. But these two components of Ekman and Friesen's classification operate predominantly by explicit communication. And since this book concentrates on the implicit: regulators, body clues, and adaptors provide one focus and one set of terminology.

An additional focus and another set of terms, though, needs to be considered so that a complete system of nonverbal, predominantly implicit communication exists before the system can be applied. Six of the seven Burgoon and Saine "codes" provide this completeness (the seventh--"body movements"--equates with, and therefore duplicates, the Ekman and Friesen classifications): (1) Physical appearance, (2) Vocalics (renamed vocal tones in this book), (3) Touch, (4) Space, (5) Time, (6) Artifacts.

(1) Physical appearance usually has an immediate--and often lasting--impact. For that reason, most authors, even within the confines of the short story, give emphasis to such items as the build, features, and adornments (clothing, accessories, and cosmetics) of their characters. Build can be divided into three basic categories technically called the endomorph, the mesomorph, and the ectomorph--less technically called the round, the trim, and the bony, respectively. Research suggests that correlations exist between build and personality and perceptions by others. An author may use build to symbolize personality. As Thomas A. Gullason points out, for example, Anton Chekhov in "Gooseberries" uses "the imagery of fatness . . . (to reveal) Nikolay's dead life; Ivan says:

'I made my way to the house and was met by a fat dog with
reddish hair that looked like a pig. It wanted to bark,
but was too lazy. The cook, a fat, barelegged woman, who
also looked like a pig, came out of the kitchen. . . . I
went in to see my brother. . . . He had grown older,

> stouter, flabby; his cheeks, his nose, his lips jutted
> out: it looked as though he might grunt . . . at any
> moment.'"[24]

John Updike is even up on the terminology itself in *Couples*: "Frank mournfully confronted the endomorph in himself. His demanding deep-socketed mistress, ectomorphic, lay relaxed at his side. . . ."[25]

Features, too, have long been considered indicators of personality traits; although physiognomy has less currency than in earlier centuries, authors still frequently depend on physical features to dramatize the essential personality of their characters: Geoffrey Chaucer's Wife of Bath is "gat-tothed"[26] to signify her boldness and lasciviousness; Philip Roth's Sheldon Grossbart in "Defender of the Faith" has "green-speckled eyes, long and narrow"[27] to signify his shiftiness and deceitfulness. Only one aspect of the features can be significantly manipulated: hair.

Authors, of course, can manipulate as they please, especially by describing the adornments of their characters. Clothing offers the most possibilities. And since clothing has been linked to personality by, among others, Christie Harris and Moira Johnston in *Figleafing Through History: The Dynamics of Dress*,[28] the robing of characters can often reveal more than disrobing. Seminars and books on dressing for success have proliferated in recent years, as the awareness of the potential of clothes to communicate through their level of formality, fit, texture, color, and so on has increased. Color choice, for example, can send messages about status and personality. There seems something particularly fitting about Hawthorne's choice of a scarlet letter for Hester Prynne, especially as the personality linked to this color is an impulsive, physical, youthful, sensual extrovert.

Other adornments have their uses, too. These include such items as jewelry, cosmetics, wigs, and the more directly functional eye glasses. Authors may choose to adorn their characters with accessories to make a point. Willa Cather gives Paul in "Paul's Case" "an opal pin in his neatly knotted black four-in-hand and a red carnation in his buttonhole." Paul makes his point to the faculty: "This latter adornment the faculty somehow felt was not properly significant of the contrite spirit befitting a boy under the ban of suspension."[29] Cather makes her point to the reader: this is no normal boy--he's a "case." Also, Cather--like many other authors--finds eye glasses an attractive adornment because they reflect not only on the literal eyesight of characters, but also on their metaphoric vision. One of Paul's many problems is a father who presents a young man as a model for Paul. But the features and sight of this young man should lead readers to see flaws in the father's choice: "This young man was of a ruddy complexion, with a compressed, red mouth, and faded, nearsighted eyes, over which he wore thick spectacles, with gold bows that curved about his ears."[30] And shortsightedness leads to and breeds more shortsightedness: he married a woman with an "angular" build, "who also wore thick glasses, and who had now borne him four children, all nearsighted like herself."[31] Overall, then, as Burgoon and Saine conclude, "Physical appearance cues . . . derive their main communication value from their strong initial impact and their possibilities for enormous variations during the course of relationship."[32]

(2) The voice has impact, too. One can listen to vocal tones without listening to the words themselves. Voice qualities and vocalizations add to or even contradict the message of the words: confident words lose their impact when spoken with a high-pitched, fast, thin voice. The most critical voice qualities are those of pitch (both its variation and level), tempo (fast or slow), amplitude (both its variation and level); vocalization features frequently depend on these qualities. A character may whisper or whine or

whimper; a character may speak in a soft (intensity), low (pitch height), drawl (extent); a character may punctuate the words of another character by a series of "uh huhs" or even by telling silences. Even the absence of voice may be significant.

Like so many other nonverbal elements, silence communicates. Yet because silence has several forms and no sounds, it can present particular interpretation difficulties. As J. Vernon Jensen puts it in his article, "Communicative Functions of Silence," "Silence can communicate scorn, hostility, coldness, defiance, sternness, and hate; but it can also communicate respect, kindness, and acceptance."[33] Silence can signal the act of thinking to some; silence can signify a lack of activity to others. Silence offers both the judgment of assent and dissent; silence generally shows assent for what is being said, but sometimes a noble silence shows dissent. Take, for example, Sir Thomas More's refusal to acknowledge Henry VIII's supremacy as head of the church. Thomas Cromwell comments on More's silence in Robert Bolt's dramatization *A Man for all Seasons*:

> CROMWELL: But, Gentlemen of the Jury, there are many kinds
> of silence. Consider first the silence of a man when he is
> dead. Let us say we go into the room where he is lying;
> and we listen. What do we hear? Silence. What does it
> betoken, this silence? Nothing. This is silence, pure and
> simple. But consider another case. Suppose I were to
> draw a dagger from my sleeve and make to kill the prisoner
> with it, and suppose their lordships there, instead of
> crying out for me to stop . . . maintained their silence.
> That *would* betoken! It would betoken a willingness that I
> should do it, and under law they would be guilty with me.
> So silence can, according to circumstances, speak.
> Consider, now, the circumstances of the prisoner's (More)
> silence. The oath was put to good and faithful subjects
> up and down the country. . . . And when it came to the

prisoner he refused. He calls this silence yet is there a man in this court, is there a man in this country, who does not *know* Sir Thomas More's opinion of the King's title? Of course not! But how can that be? Because this silence betokened--nay, this silence *was* not silence at all but most eloquent denial.[34]

Context, then, is again the key to resolving many apparent uncertainties. Burgoon and Saine record numerous other theories about the roles of silence--all of which echo its complexity.

Authors make use of both silence and sound. Sometimes, they simply suggest through a seemingly casual mention of voice quality or change; sometimes, they shout out the meaning of a voice's sound. Norman Mailer--no stranger to shouting out--has Stephen Rojack in *An American Dream* first use build, then adornment, then features, and finally--loudest of all--voice to describe Deborah, his wife:

She was a handsome woman, Deborah, she was big. With high heels she stood at least an inch over me. She had a huge mass of black hair and striking green eyes sufficiently arrogant and upon occasion sufficiently amused to belong to a queen. She had a large Irish nose and a wide mouth which took many shapes, but her complexion was her claim to beauty. . . . It was her voice however which seduced one first. Her face was large and all-but-honest; her voice was a masterwork of treachery. Clear as a bell, yet slithery with innuendo, it leaped like a deer, slipped like a snake. She could not utter a sentence for giving a tinkle of value to some innocent word. It may have been the voice of a woman you would not trust for an instant, but I did not know if I could forget it.[35]

He couldn't. Not after he murdered her. Rojack touches his wife with death: he pushes her out the window.

(3) Touch, however, can communicate in less deadly ways. Touch, the mother of the senses, developed in the womb and remains a biological necessity. Our culture, though, places certain taboos on touch right from infancy. This touch deprivation can lead to physical problems: for example, infant death, allergies, and eczema;[36] psychological difficulties: for example, those deprived of touch can grow up being verbally and physically hostile--as Ashley Montagu says, "Such persons rub others the wrong way because they have been failed in the experience of being stroked the right way";[37] and cultural differences: for example, "Cultures that display a lot of physical affection toward infants have a low incidence of theft, murder, rape, and physical punishment, while those that deny physical pleasure to infants generally have high rates of adult violence."[38] In one sense these are all problems of communication--the failure of some to communicate love to others.

Touch and love go together in intimate relationships, too: touch can arouse. Montagu suggests, though, that many sexual problems have their origins in childhood tactile deprivation. At the other end of the scale from intimate touch stands formal touch--the handshake, the greeting kiss, and so on. Formal touch attempts to substitute for other culturally taboo touches. Of all the nonverbal codes, touch as a communication code seems the least understood. Despite its potential ambiguity when used alone, though, touch can help clarify certain nonverbal messages when used with other codes: a slap, for instance, delivered with a playful facial expression. Further, certain self-touch actions (which would also fit Ekman's "body manipulator" category) clearly indicate attempts to relieve tension. Montagu reports that rubbing the thumb and index finger together and rubbing all the fingers against the palm of the hand are general tension-relieving signs. But signs specific to each gender exist, too. Men scratch their heads, rub their chins or forehead or cheeks or back of the neck, and tug their ear lobes; women put a finger on their lower front teeth with their mouths slightly open or place a finger under their chins.[39]

Authors use the touch code both to suggest tension and other emotions in individual characters and to clarify relationships. Montagu cites an example from literature to illuminate his point that the loss of touch from separate bed marriages results in couples growing "out of touch" with one another. Alma in Lillian Smith's *Strange Fruit* reflects:

> Sometimes all she could remember of hers and Tut's nights together was the lifting of his leg off her body. There was something almost *dissipated* about the way Tut slept, letting himself go, so, so uncontrolled, you might say. Alma had thought of twin beds but had never done anything about it, for she doubted in her heart that husbands and wives should sleep separately. It was all a little vague to her, but sleeping together, cold weather or hot, seemed a necessary thread in the fabric of marriage, which, once broken, might cause the whole thing to unravel.
>
> Just how she was not certain. She was convinced, however, that her own mother's custom of sleeping in a room separate from father's had caused their family life to be not as successful as it should have been.[40]

What Alma fears is a change in space--a change which would make touch impossible and distance, physical and psychological, probable.

(4) Space communicates. Alma in moving from a double-bed to a single bed would also move out of Edward T. Hall's "intimate distance" (up to eighteen inches), out of sharing a bubble with her husband into her own protective bubble of personal distance (between eighteen and forty-eight inches): she would move away from receiving his senses--"heat from the body,

tactile stimulation from the skin, the fragrance of perfume, even the sound of breathing"[41]--to a distance where sight dominates the sense of space. Hall categorizes two further zones of space in North American culture: social and public. Impersonal relations, such as those which occur at work or during business transactions, seem to take place at a "social distance" (from four to twelve feet). Public addresses, such as those by a teacher or a politician, take place at a "public distance" (more than twelve feet). Distance also influences other dimensions of communication such as vocal tones and vision. Whereas whispering works at an intimate distance, shouting succeeds at a public distance; whereas the whole body can be seen communicating from a personal and a social distance, this does not always hold true for intimate distance (too close) or public distance (too far). Henry David Thoreau's experiment in living at Walden made him particularly conscious that his situation enabled there to be "commonly sufficient space. . . . Our horizon is never quite at our elbows."[42] Furthermore, he came to realize, and record in comic-serious fashion, the relationship between vocal tones and distance:

> One inconvenience I sometimes experienced in so small a house, the difficulty of getting to a sufficient distance from my guest when we began to utter the big thoughts in big words. You want room for your thoughts to get into sailing trim and run a course or two before they make their port. The bullet of your thought must have overcome its lateral and ricochet motion and fallen into its last and steady course before it reaches the ear of the hearer, else it may plow out again through the side of his head. Also, our sentences wanted room to unfold. . . . Individuals, like nations, must have suitable broad and natural boundaries, even a considerable neutral ground, between them. I found it a singular luxury to talk across the pond to a companion on the opposite side. In my house we were so near that we could not begin to hear,--we could

not speak low enough to be heard. . . . If we are merely loquacious and loud talkers, then we can afford to stand very near together, cheek by jowl, and feel each other's breath; but if we speak reservedly and thoughtfully, we want to be farther apart, that all animal heat and moisture may have a chance to evaporate. . . . Speech is for the convenience of those who are hard of hearing; but there are many fine things which we cannot say if we have to shout. As the conversation began to assume a loftier and grander tone, we gradually shoved our chairs farther apart till they touched the wall in opposite corners, and then commonly there was not room enough.[43]

Thoreau entertains visitors in his own territory. With perhaps the exception of the automobile, territory doesn't move. It can, however, be manipulated so as to reveal status and dominance (for example, the size and location of an office and the positioning of the furniture within that office). Violation of territorial rights--even in such seemingly public places as a certain chair in a library, or in a classroom, or in a park--can be most threatening. To avoid such violations, people build permanent barriers (such as fences) or place temporary markers (such as books) to indicate the boundaries of territory.

Thoreau's feeling "sufficient space" comes in a chapter titled "Solitude," a chapter which speaks to his sense of territory. His reservation about "sufficient distance" comes in a chapter titled "Visitors," a chapter which reflects his sense of personal space. Just as territorial rights can be violated, so can personal space rights. As W. H. Auden warns:

Some thirty inches from my nose
The frontier of my Person goes,
And all the untilled air between
Is private pagus or demesne.
Stranger, unless with bedroom eyes
I beckon you to fraternize,

> Beware of rudely crossing it:
> I have no gun, but I can spit.[44]

His individual comic-poetic hostility reflects a documented truth. When personal space dwindles, people frequently protect themselves by drawing away, or by tensing muscles, or by placing artifacts (such as a briefcase) between themselves and others, or by hiding behind furniture. When personal space disappears, people become anxious and attempt to withdraw. The way authors position characters in relation to other characters and to territorial rights helps readers infer the relationships among characters, their emotional status, their social status, and their dominance.

(5) Time frequently relates to space and to the other codes. Hall opens his book *The Silent Language* by asserting, "Time talks . . . it can shout the truth where words lie."[45] Status and dominance can be established not just by size and organization of an office, but also by lengthening the waiting period outside the office for a visitor. Of all the nonverbal codes, time may have the most definite yet most misunderstood cultural distinctions. In South America, for instance, time is generally treated leisurely, and a number of activities can be conducted simultaneously. But in North America time is generally viewed as monochronistic, with urgency, and through activity. Normally, North Americans schedule one activity at a time; deviating from that norm (for example, by reading when someone is talking to us) communicates uninterest. Part of the urgency comes from regarding time in economic terms, since we "buy" time, "save" time, "spend" time, "waste" time, "make" time.

Another part of the urgency of time comes from the awareness that time steadily steps off the inevitable march toward death. To slow that march down, Joseph Heller's character Dunbar in *Catch-22* engages in boring activities: "Dunbar loved shooting skeet because he hated every minute of it and the time passed so slowly. He had figured out that a single hour on the skeet-shooting range with people like Havermeyer and Appleby could be worth as much as eleven-times-seventeen years."[46] Dunbar is both typical and atypical. Typical because he seeks activity; as Burgoon and Saine conclude: "Americans feel that we must always be doing something lest we communicate that we are unambitious, lazy, and wasting time."[47] Atypical because he seeks an activity that he does not enjoy. In his own way, Dunbar often manages to be an incisive philosopher about informal time:

> "Do you know how long a year takes when it's going away?"
> Dunbar repeated to Clevinger. "This long." He snapped
> his fingers. "A second ago you were stepping into
> college. . . . Today you're an old man. . . . You're
> inches away from death every time you go on a mission.
> How much older can you be at your age? A half minute
> before that you were stepping into high school. . . .
> Only a fifth of a second before that you were a small kid
> with a ten-week summer vacation that lasted a hundred
> thousand years and still ended too soon."[48]

Informal time, time without the steady beat of the clock, equals mental time. Formal time, measured in subdivisions of seconds and centuries, controls public lives and consequently communicates. Take a scheduled, clock-determined appointment. To most people, arriving early indicates eagerness; arriving late displays disdain; not arriving at all reveals disinterest. To be punctual is to follow timidly the cultural norm and breaking such norms often is interpreted as an act of rudeness or sloppiness. That formal time in of itself is an artificial measure seems of little consequence in our attitudes towards it.

The effects of time attitudes on the mind and on the memory can play a devastating part in scarring the psyche. John Steinbeck articulates one impact of memorable time in *East of Eden:*

> Time interval is a strange and contradictory matter in the mind. It would be reasonable to suppose that a routine time or an eventless time would seem interminable. It should be so, but it is not. It is the dull eventless times that have no duration whatever. A time splashed with interest, wounded with tragedy, crevassed with joy--that's the time that seems long in the memory. And this is right when you think about it. Eventlessness has no posts to drape duration on. From nothing to nothing is no time at all.[49]

Time is a code all the time.

(6) Artifacts comprise Burgoon and Saine's final, catchall code. By artifacts they primarily mean environment and objects--fertile grounds for conventional symbols. Artifacts communicate in two ways. First, environment and objects--for example, a room and its furnishings--can provide "information about the person's preferences, interests, and habits." Second, "people's attitudes and behavior are frequently influenced by their environment";[50] attitudes and behavior influence communication. And many factors contribute toward the total environment, ranging from lines to lighting, from temperature to texture, from sound to other sensory stimulations. Inside and outside, we react--often unknowingly--to the environment about us.

Of all the Ekman and Friesen classifications and the Burgoon and Saine codes, "objects and environment" is the most recognized of the nonverbal elements by analyzers of literature--although under the less obtrusive but more general heading of "setting." Authors and readers seem particularly aware of this aspect and examples of setting and articles that map setting

23

abound. In some fiction, the setting functions as a natural backdrop. Sometimes, however, the setting takes on almost supernatural proportions and functions rather like another character. Thomas Hardy's Egdon Heath in *The Return of the Native* stands out as perhaps the most notable example. The heath imposes its overshadowing expanse and affects all the characters in the novel.

In other fiction, the setting reflects as well as affects the values of the characters. This occurs in manmade environments like Updike's supermarket in "A & P." Not only does Updike design the interior of the store with its "cat-and-dog-food-breakfast-cereal-macaroni-rice-raisins-seasonings-spreads-spaghetti-soft-drinks-crackers-and-cookies aisle" and populate it with "house-slaves in pin curlers" appearing out of aisles like a ball in "a pinball machine," but he also plants the supermarket in the exterior world. This store with its mundane middle-class values stands in the middle of a town north of Boston within sight of "two banks and the Congregational church and the newspaper store and three real-estate offices."[51] The setting, the company's rather pretentious full name (The Atlantic and Pacific Tea Company), and the values inside and outside the supermarket, all guide our response to Sammy's confused and questionable motives in turning in his company-issued bow tie.

Setting has received considerable attention, even to the point of developing complex systems to describe setting. This is not surprising since we either recognize settings in literature or travel to them vicariously. What is surprising, though, is that all the other classifications and codes described have received scant attention and have been inadequately applied to the study of literature. Yet understanding a character or the point of a piece of literature may well hinge on our sensitivity to a nonverbal occurence. Some, perhaps, have believed it to be a too expansive and too elusive approach for any one study. They have taken a restrictive approach by isolating a particular aspect (time, for example) and exploring how a particular author uses such an aspect (often in just a single work). Their approach has the value of focus but the limitation of isolating a single code that operates intimately, simultaneously, and revealingly with other codes. The expansive approach taken here invites readers of literature--and specifically readers of the short story--to notice all implicit nonverbal details implanted by authors and to transplant these into patterns of meaning.

This pattern of meaning may only become clear after a detailed examination of the total nonverbal elements in a work of literature. The three Ekman and Friesen terms and the six Burgoon and Saine codes provide the necessary framework for such a complete examination. Each of these elements can be separated--but not isolated--and noted when reading a work of literature. What soon becomes evident from such an approach is that many of the elements are interdependent. Vocal tones and body clues, for example, frequently intersect: an angry tone of voice can either be confirmed or denied by a facial expression.

Sometimes, authors leave nothing to chance and explicitly interpret the nonverbal. Updike provides an example in his novel *Rabbit, Run* when he tells readers that Mr. Springer's "painfully complex smile" signifies "a wish to apologize for his wife (we're both men; I know), a wish to keep distant (nevertheless you've behaved unforgivably; don't touch me), and the car salesman's mechanical reflex of politeness."[52] But more often, authors create the nonverbal inconspicuously as part of the overall intricate design of detail--a blueprint too frequently examined only in its parts, too important to continue virtually unnoticed.

Notes

[1] Henry James, "The Art of Fiction," in *Partial Portraits* (Ann Arbor: Univ. of Michigan Press, 1970), p. 388.

[2] James, p. 389.

[3] James, p. 393.

[4] Paul Ekman, Wallace V. Friesen, John Bear, "The International Language of Gesture," *Psychology Today*, May 1984, p. 64.

[5] Kenneth Burke, *Language as Symbolic Action: Essays on Life, Literature, and Method* (Berkeley: Univ. of California Press, 1966), p. 420.

[6] Judee K. Burgoon and Thomas Saine, *The Unspoken Dialogue: An Introduction to Nonverbal Communication* (Boston: Houghton Mifflin, 1978), p. 22.

[7] T.S. Eliot, *The Sacred Wood: Essays on Poetry and Criticism* (London: Methuen, 1950), p. 100.

[8] Ernest Hemingway, *A Moveable Feast* (New York: Charles Scribner's Sons, 1964), p. 75.

[9] Ekman and Friesen, "Nonverbal Leakage and Clues to Deception," *Psychiatry*, 32 (1969), 88-106.

[10] J.D. Salinger, "For Esme--With Love and Squalor," in *Nine Stories* (Boston: Little, Brown, 1948), p. 146.

[11] Salinger, p. 140.

[12] Salinger, p. 153.

[13] Salinger, p. 153.

[14] Stephen Crane, *Maggie: A Girl of the Streets*, in *Bowery Tales*, ed. Fredson Bowers (Charlottesville: The Univ. Press of Virginia, 1969), p. 67.

[15] Edward T. Hall, *Beyond Culture* (Garden City, N.Y.: Anchor Books, 1976), p. 37.

[16] Edward Sapir, "The Unconscious Patterning of Behavior in Society," in *The Unconscious: A Symposium*, ed. E.S. Drummer (New York: Alfred A. Knopf, 1927), pp. 114-42. Reprinted in *Selected Writings of Edward Sapir in Language, Culture and Personality*, ed. David E. Mandelbaum (Berkeley: University of California Press, 1949), p. 556.

[17] Albert Mehrabian, *Nonverbal Communication* (Chicago: Aldine Atherton, 1972), p.2.

[18] Randall P. Harrison, "Nonverbal Communication," in *Handbook of Communications*, eds. I. de Sola Pool, et al. (Chicago: Rand McNally, 1973), p. 93.

[19] Ekman and Friesen, "The Repertoire of Nonverbal Behavior: Categories, Origins, Usage and Coding,"*Semiotics* 1 (1969), 48-98; Burgoon and Saine, p. 5 and chapters three and four.

[20] Michael Argyle, *Bodily Communication* (New York: International Universities Press, 1975), pp. 160-67.

[21] Ekman and Friesen, "The Repertoire," p. 82.

[22] Flannery O'Connor, "Good Country People," in *The Complete Stories* (New York: Farrar, Straus and Giroux, 1975), p. 278.

[23] Ekman, "Biological and Cultural Contributions to Body and Facial Movement," in *The Anthropology of the Body*, ed. John Blacking (London: Academic Press, 1977), pp. 46-47.

[24] Thomas A. Gullason, "The Short Story: An Underrated Art,"*Studies in Short Fiction*, 2 (Fall 1964), 13-31; rpt. in *Short Story Theories*, ed. Charles E. May (Athens: Ohio Univ. Press, 1976), p. 26.

[25] John Updike, *Couples* (New York: Alfred A. Knopf, 1968), p. 115.

[26] Geoffrey Chaucer, *The Canterbury Tales*, in *The Works of Geoffrey Chaucer*, ed. F.N. Robinson, 2nd ed. (Boston: Houghton Mifflin, 1957), p. 21. See also note to line 468 on p. 663.

[27] Philip Roth, "Defender of The Faith," in *Goodbye Columbus and Five Short Stories* (Boston: Houghton Mifflin, 1959), p. 163.

[28] Christie Harris and Moira Johnston, *Figleafing Through History: The Dynamics of Dress* (New York: Atheneum, 1972).

[29] Willa Cather, "Paul's Case," in *Troll Garden* (Lincoln: Univ. of Nebraska Press, 1983), p. 102.

[30] Cather, p. 109.

[31] Cather, p. 109.

[32] Burgoon and Saine, p. 80.

[33] J. Vernon Jensen, "Communicative Functions of Silence," *ETC.: A Review of General Semantics* 30 (1973), 252. See also pp. 249-57.

[34] Robert Bolt, *A Man For All Seasons* (New York: Random House, 1962), pp. 151-152.

[35] Norman Mailer, *An American Dream* (New York: The Dial Press, 1965), pp. 19-20.

[36] See, for example, W.J. O'Donovan, *Dermatological Neuroses* (London: Kegan Paul, 1927); M.E. Obermayer, *Psychocutaneous Medicine* (Springfield, Ill.: Charles C. Thomas, 1966).

[37] Ashley Montagu, *Touching: The Human Significance of the Skin* (New York: Columbia University Press, 1971), p. 275.

[38] Burgoon and Saine, p. 68.

[39] Montagu, *Touching*, pp. 208-09.

[40] Lillian Smith, *Strange Fruit* (New York: Reynal, 1944), p. 74. See also Montagu, pp. 248-50. Interestingly, this literary example and many others are offered by researchers in the nonverbal, along with empirical research and data, as evidence of some aspect of the nonverbal.

[41] Edward and Mildred Hall, "The Sounds of Silence," *Playboy*, June 1971, p. 148. See also pp. 138, 139, 148, 204, 206, and Edward T. Hall, *The Hidden Dimension* (Garden City, N.Y.: Anchor Books, 1969).

[42] Henry David Thoreau, *Walden*, ed. J. Lyndon Shanley (Princeton, N.J.: Princeton Univ. Press, 1971), p. 130.

[43] Thoreau, pp. 140-41.

[44] W.H. Auden, "Thanksgiving for a Habitat, "*W. H. Auden Collected Poems*, ed. Edward Mendelson (New York: Random House, 1976), p. 519. See also Hall, *The Hidden Dimension*, chapter 8.

[45] Hall, *The Silent Language* (Garden City, N.J.: Doubleday, 1959), p. 23.

[46] Joseph Heller, *Catch-22* (New York: Simon and Schuster, 1955), pp. 37-38.

[47] Burgoon and Saine, p. 101.

[48] Heller, pp. 38-39.

[49] John Steinbeck, *East of Eden* (New York: The Viking Press, 1952), p. 55.

[50] Burgoon and Saine, p. 101.

[51] John Updike, "A & P," in *Pigeon Feathers and Other Stories* (New York: Alfred A. Knopf, 1969), pp. 190-92.

[52] John Updike, *Rabbit, Run* (New York: Alfred A. Knopf, 1960), p. 200.

Chapter 2
THE SHORT-CHANGED SHORT STORY

"The Flash of Fireflies."

Nadine Gordimer.

This blueprint can be used for any genre. In a comprehensive nonverbal approach, the reader systematically searches for each of the nine elements, seeks to make connections among them, and ultimately, with the help of the nonverbal research, settles on meanings. Such a comprehensive approach is critical, whatever the genre, because certain of these elements so often function together: an angry person both looks and sounds angry.

The Ekman and Friesen classification of regulators, body clues, and adaptors provide three of the benchmarks, focusing as they do on primarily implicit communication occurring from the physical presence of individuals. The Burgoon and Saine codes of physical appearance, vocal tones, touch, space, time and artifacts provide the other six benchmarks, focusing as they do on primarily implicit communication occurring by several means--not all of which require the presence of the encoder. Thus these nine benchmarks and the accompanying nonverbal research can enable the reader to identify and to comprehend the many nonverbal moments in literature.

All four major genres (poem, play, novel, short story) have already received some analysis based on our knowledge of nonverbal communication. But so often such analysis has been too fragmentary to convince readers that the nonverbal may often be at least as important as the verbal. To examine one element in isolation, often in a single work, results in too many lines being left off the blueprint for it to be useful. Indeed, a comprehensive approach can add more than just an understanding of a particular work. It can add to our understanding of the genres themselves. In fact, one justification for separating the short story and the novel from the frequent unigenre of "fiction" comes from the distinctive uses of nonverbal moments in these two types of literature.

Of the four genres listed, poetry has received the least attention by those critics interested in the nonverbal. R. P. Blackmur's tantalizingly titled book *Language as Gesture: Essays in Poetry* begins with the real promise of something new but continues, concludes, and fades away with essays (many of them earlier essays) that wander from the focus of the first chapter. But in that fascinating first essay, Blackmur does provide an important perspective on gesture (which he leaves largely undefined) in the arts generally and in poems specifically.

This relatively early (1942), eclectic, and eloquent essay touches on a number of nonverbal points not formalized by others until many years later. Blackmur mentions, for example, both environment (in his section on architecture: "We feel that pillars are mighty, that a bridge spans or leaps, that a dome covers us, or a crypt appalls us"[1]) and clothing (in his section on dancing: "It is the costumes of a ballet that determine what the gestures shall be, as the cut of one's cloth determines one's stride"[2]). From columns and costumes, he moves to canvas and in one bold stroke asserts that the great portrait painter uses texture and light to capture the "vital gesture of the single focal moment"[3] rather than the overall, average effect projected through several sittings. The great sculptor, too, fashions "movement arrested, in the moving stillness, there is a gesture completed at the moment of its greatest significance. . . . Sculpture is man breeding shapes out of his brooding."[4]   Then Blackmur's lyricism strikes another note as he sings that "the purpose of music is to create gestures of the human spirit."[5]

The great writer, to Blackmur, moves beyond recording generalities into capturing gestures: the writer without gestures is merely a stenographer.   In fiction, Blackmur senses that "the stress and urgency of plot. . . determines *what* gestures are wanted and by its exigencies *when* they shall be released."[6]   In poetry, Blackmur feels that the very use of language can create the effect of gesture, that the techniques of repetition, alliteration, punning, and refraining can be "pushed to the condition of gesture."[7]   To the great poet, "gestures are the first steps toward the making of symbols, and those symbols which endure are the residuary legatees of the meanings earned through gesture."[8]

Clearly, a nonverbal approach to reading poetry would have uneven results.   But, as Blackmur suggests, there lurks beneath the surface of the words a collective meaning.   Perhaps in no other genre is the reader made to work so hard to discover that meaning.   But a poet's use of nonverbal elements often comes closest to that of the short story writer, where moments are often momentous.

Certain types of poetry lend themselves more obviously to a nonverbal approach.   One only has to think of several Robert Browning dramatic monologues, for example, to recognize this.   In "My Last Duchess," the reader not only imagines the Duke's variable vocal tones and body clues, but also realizes that the Duke has interpreted (usually incorrectly) the body clues of his last Duchess; her smiles proved fatal.   His inability to decode her ready smiles comes as no surprise.   The nonverbal research demonstrates our relative inaccuracy in decoding, especially if the context complicates matters; the Duke's jealousy blinds him to more than her smiles.   In the dramatic monologue, the reader also contemplates the listener.   Although silent, the listener gives body clues. Andrea Del Sarto's wife undoubtedly listens to her painter husband's pitiful monologue in "Andrea Del Sarto" with considerable boredom and occasional distraction, showing clear signs of wanting to leave to go to her lover.

The dramatic monologue, then, is a play of poetry in the minor key of a significant moment. A full-fledged drama often carries the form of a poetic play in the major key of stormy lives. Nowhere is this more true than in the work of Shakespeare. Interestingly, the majority of Blackmur's examples come from Shakespeare's plays. For one thing, Shakespeare as a man of theatre not only understood the importance of the nonverbal of the stage, but also articulated this importance on the page, as, for example, through Desdemona in *Othello*: "I understand a fury in your words/But not the words."[9]

Furthermore, drama would seem to be the most natural genre to discuss the nonverbal. Not so. For one thing, Western theatre and Western dramas rarely dictate the expressive movements of actors. Certainly such movement exists. Indeed, Jonathon Miller in "Plays and Players" intimates that the impact of film with its ability to zoom in on the tiniest of features and its capacity to capture even the softest whisper has led to more subtle nonverbal expressions by actors (many of whom double in both media) faced by more nonverbally sophisticated and demanding audiences (many of whom are devotees of both media). Miller also emphasizes that most Western actors consciously construct most of their expressive movements in rehearsal; the existence of a studied script makes the origin of the nonverbal nonsimultaneous yet nonprescribed in Western drama.[10]

But as with so many aspects of the nonverbal such elements are culturally determined. Macdonald Critchley in his chapter on "The Oriental Theatre" in *The Language of Gesture* points out that in Eastern "Stage-craft the drama is so precise that the gestures are as fixed as a musical score. Nothing is left to chance and the actor will no more yield to impulse in a spontaneous gesture than in an interpolated line."[11] Whereas Eastern theatre opens its doors to systematic nonverbal analysis, Western theatre offers only a limited run to such an analysis on a performance by performance basis.

This has not always been the case, however. In "Inversion, Parody, and Irony: The Visual Rhetoric of Renaissance English Tragedy," Huston Diehl traces the development of iconography from Tudor morality plays to later Renaissance tragedies. He clearly demonstrates the importance of the visual in such drama and illustrates the shared knowledge between actor and audience of the symbolic meaning of various visuals. Hand properties, physical features, costumes, and actions were all icons used to externalize to the audience the inner struggles of the characters.

Three of these icons--physical features, costumes, and actions--continue today to be of symbolic importance. But as Diehl has shown, even in the period from Tudor morality plays to Renaissance tragedies, "Iconic, visual detail becomes increasingly implicit, subtle, and submerged in the realistic action of the mature tragedies. . . ."[12] And, on occasion, icons become ironic. Othello rather than Iago is black (the icon of the devil); the strawberry-spotted handkerchief serves not only plot purposes (if that were its only purpose, it would be a rather weak contrivance), but also as an ironic icon: strawberries symbolizing deceit and the handkerchief around the head symbolizing spiritual disease.[13] In the centuries since Shakespeare, symbolic connections have tended to become even more implicit, subtle, and submerged.

Dramatic irony, however, remains an important technique. Tom Stoppard's television play *Professional Foul,* for instance, centers around ethical questions confused by the ambiguity of communication. A moment of delicious nonverbal irony occurs when Professor Anderson, distracted by his thoughts of a dissident seeking his assistance,[14] gets up to leave during a session at a Philosophy conference. The Chairman of the session mistakes Anderson's move as a signal that he has a comment to make on the paper just delivered. Anderson finds words: "Language is not the only level of human communication, and perhaps not the most important level. Whereof we cannot speak, thereof we are by no means silent. (McKendrick smiles 'Bravo.')"[15] The very man who minutes before started to sneak out then delivers his final truth: "The essentials of a given situation speak for themselves, and language is as capable of obscuring the truth as of revealing it."[16] Having covered his tracks with language, Anderson leaves. The television camera today zooms to magnify modern irony, where once icons served. But in both cases, the audience needs to be alert beyond dialogue.

This is also true with the novel. As many of the literary examples already used illustrate, the novel needs the nonverbal. And yet the subject of implicit nonverbal communication in the novel has received largely periferal treatment. One teasing encounter is Paul A. Eschholz's "Mark Twain and the Language of Gesture."[17] Although Eschholz, like Blackmur, Miller, Critchley, and others, avoids specific classification and codification by sheltering under the broad umbrella of "gesture," he does establish Twain's extensive use and expansive knowledge of the nonverbal. In *A Connecticut Yankee in King Arthur's Court*, for instance, Twain, through Hank Morgan, reveals his sensitivity to the real language of truth:

> I watched my fifty-two boys narrowly; watched their faces, their walk, their unconscious attitudes; for all these are language--a language given us purposely that it may betray us in times of emergency, when we have secrets which we want to keep.[18]

One of the most amusing of these betrayals in all of Twain comes, as Eschholz

points out, in *Adventures of Huckleberry Finn* when the observant Mrs. Loftus

demolishes Huck's girl disguise:

> You do a girl tolerable poor, but you might fool men,
> maybe. Bless you, child, when you set out to thread a
> needle, don't hold the thread still and fetch the needle
> up to it; hold the needle still and poke the thread at
> it--that's the way a woman most always does; but a man
> always does t'other way. And when you throw at a rat or
> anything, hitch yourself up a tip-toe, and fetch your hand
> up over your head as awkward as you can, and miss your rat
> about six or seven foot. Throw stiff-armed from the
> shoulder, like there was a pivot there for it to turn on,
> like a girl; not from the wrist and elbow, with your arm
> out to one side, like a boy. And mind you, when a girl
> tries to catch anything in her lap, she throws her knees
> apart; she don't clap them together, the way you did when
> you catched the lump of lead.[19]

Twain noticed what later research confirmed: many and specific gender

differences exist in both nonverbal encoding and decoding. Eschholz also

cites Hank Morgan's comments on the disparity between King Arthur's posture

and his clothes in *A Connecticut Yankee in King Arthur's Court* and discusses

in detail how David Wilson in *The Tragedy of Pudd'nhead Wilson* makes Tom

Driscoll confess to murder nonverbally.

Had Eschholz gone beyond the half-a-dozen authors on the nonverbal that

he mentions and had he refined the terms he seems to use so interchangeably

("gesture," "kinesics," "nonverbal," "body motions," "body language"), he

might well have established another way of reading Twain. As it is, he has

taken the first tentative step by suggesting that novelists like Twain use

nonverbal communication because it "not only complements verbal communication in a narrative, but also enriches the entire literary experience for the sensitive reader."[20] He concludes that the nonverbal accomplishes a number of functions in fiction because it is "not only. . . more focused and succinct than often cumbersome dialogue, but also leaves an unmistakable or indelible impression of particular characters with the reader. In addition, it can function thematically as it does with Twain's favorite theme of appearance and reality, and it can heighten interest, suspense, and realism in a dramatic scene."[21] It does all these things. But Eschholz frustratingly leaves us only with a glossy picturebook featuring a few unlinked examples from a single author; he does not offer us a clear mapbook from which we can plot our way through any author's use of all of the nonverbal routes.

Other critics also take a rather limited approach, although sometimes they provide fascinating glimpses. One such work is Frances Freeman Paden's "Autistic Gestures in *The Heart is a Lonely Hunter*." Paden discusses gestures that characters direct to themselves that appear irrelevant to the situations existing. In particular, she focuses on the way Carson McCullers draws attention to hands in the novel. The major characters turn ever inward with their anger as first verbal communication fails them then nonverbal communication disintegrates. Instead of absorbing all forms of communications from others, the major characters begin to reflect them and to express their frustration by hitting themselves in a flurry of autistic blows. Singer, Blount, Copeland, Kelly, and Brannon, although they all "seem to reach out to others,. . . are, in fact, trying to get in touch with themselves."[22] Paden notices McCullers' use of touch and manipulators, claiming that the latter goes beyond the normal bounds into the psychological territory of autistic gesture. However defined, these nonverbal actions contribute significantly to our understanding of this novel.

The problem with applying a comprehensive nonverbal approach to the novel, though, comes from the sheer length of the form. And although, as Eschholz points out, the novel benefits from the nonverbal moments by becoming "more focused and succinct," it does not depend on them in the same way as the short story does. Indeed, a better understanding of the use of the nonverbal in the short story could go a long way in helping to redefine the genre. For externally, the short story suffers from an identity crisis. And internally, the short story could certainly be enriched by more attention to the role of the nonverbal.

First, that identity crisis. Author after author in the fine collection of essays in *Short Story Theories* complains that the short story has at best been underrated, at worst ignored. They testify that the genre runs "a poor fourth to poetry, drama, and novel-length fiction in the books and journals devoted to serious theoretical criticism";[23] even its name seems endangered-- threatened by the all-embracing, less-discerning title of "fiction." Why this crisis? Some believe that two "heroes" of the genre had too large an impact, that the short story became enslaved to Edgar Allan Poe and O. Henry. Poe's notion of the "single effect" has, to Norman Friedman at least, become an overly emphasized "fossil survivor of Poe's aesthetic" that "confuses whole- ness with singleness, unity with intensity."[24] O. Henry's success with rather formulaic plots spawned a legion of imitators. Charles E. May suggests that the relative dearth of current criticism on the short story "is largely a reaction to too much systematic criticism in the first few decades of the twentieth century when the form became solidified by rules";[25] yet another fossil. Even to this day, Friedman feels, the short story is tainted by commercialism and damned by condescension."[26] A consensus forms that the short story desperately needs more theoretical considerations--especially in matters of technique.

The use of the nonverbal is a technique--a technique conceived in "the ability to see the ordinary extraordinarily well"[27] and delivered as, in Eudora Welty's words, "the rippling texture of surface in running water and flowing air . . . the palpable shadows and colored reflections . . . the matter that mirrored the reality."[28] Reality is the mirror of the miniature. And the short story evolves out of--and revolves around--the miniature. As Gullason warns, "the reader must be thoroughly awake from the opening word" of a short story because, unlike the novel which affords several opportunities to crystallize characters and ideas, the short story operates through the momentary, through "the poetry of 'much in little.'"[29] Whereas the novelist can send out long and recurrent beams of light like a lighthouse, the short story writer sends out "The Flash of Fireflies."[30]

Readers have to be ready to catch the flash, to become, in Robert Portune's phrase, "collaborators anonymous."[31] In the novel such collaboration is often minimal. H. E. Bates suggests that novelists like Charles Dickens underestimated the reader by providing exhaustive character descriptions "by the system of catalogue," a catalogue that Dickens "reissued . . . after an interval in which he judged the reader might have forgotten what goods were for sale."[32] This was all very well for a lengthy novel addressed to a contemporary audience, but Bates claims that too many short story writers tried the same technique which "was rather like dressing a six-months-old baby in a top-hat and fur coat, with the inevitable result--suffocation."[33] The change in mobility and sophistication of the reader of the short story brought it the necessary whiff of oxygen and changed the genre because it became "no longer necessary to describe; it is enough to suggest. The full length portrait, in full dress, with scenic background, has become superfluous; now it is enough that we should know a woman by the shape of her hands."[34] But do we always notice hands and those other muted authorial fingerprints?

Bates quite correctly and most fluently states the importance of the seemingly minor in the short story. Nor is he alone. A. E. Coppard comments that the great short story writers have "the art of telling a story by a series of subtly implied gestures, swift shots, moments of suggestion";[35] Gullason says that such writers "write in short hand; and one word, a phrase, can raise the short story to a new level of meaning";[36] James Hilton claims these writers blow "you a petal of meaning instead of felling the whole forest for you."[37] But readers still have to recognize those suggestions, transcribe that short hand, and catch this petal. Sometimes they're so fleeting. Hilton's petal becomes Bates's dirty paper as Bates gives examples and identifies the importance of a perceptive audience:

> That scrap of dirty paper blown by wind along the empty
> morning street, a girl sewing, on a railway station, the
> tear in her lover's jacket and he hiding it by holding up
> a suitcase, a mother staring dumbly at her returned
> gangster son--these tiny moments, seen as it were tele-
> scopically, brightly focused, unelaborated and unex-
> plained, stamp swiftly on the mind the impressions of
> desolation, embarrassed love, or maternal despair. Each
> moment implies something it does not state; each sends out
> a swift brief signal on a certain emotional wave-length,
> relying on the attuned mental apparatus of the audience to
> pick it up.[38]

Therein lies one rub. To collaborate fully, readers need to be in tune. And yet because those aspects of the nonverbal most useful to literary inter- pretation (the three Ekman and Friesen elements plus the six Burgoon and Saine codes) function primarily below full consciousness in characters and usually beyond the explicit statements of authors, the nonverbal elements may well be misinterpreted or even missed altogether. For readers have rarely been afforded either the necessary "mental apparatus" to fill in the ellipsis or to understand the warts[39] and wrinkles that appear on the face of the short story--and are its heart.

Time and again, hopeful critics of the short story, bolstered by the illusion that New Criticism skills not only suffice but permeate all readers, depend on readers to have at their fingertips a conscious as well as unconscious grasp of the nonverbal. A. L. Bader, for instance, admiringly quotes L. A. G. Strong:

> The modern short story writer is content if, allowing the reader to glance at his characters as through a window, he shows them making a gesture which is typical: . . . a gesture which enables the reader's imagination to fill in all that is left unsaid. Instead of giving us a finished action to admire, or pricking the bubble of some problem, he may give us only the key-piece of a mosaic, around which, if sufficiently perceptive we can see in shadowy outline the completed pattern.[40]

But Bader glides past and glosses over the critical phrase: "if sufficiently perceptive."

Other short story critics have a limited recognition of the need to provide that mental apparatus necessary to reduce the number of ifs and to spotlight that key piece of mosaic. Their vision is limited because they, like some of their counterpart critics of the novel, treat the nonverbal in fragments. Rust Hills, for example, in *Writing in General and the Short Story in Particular* stresses how characters act nonverbally in a stress situation, but he goes no further.[41] James W. Gargano glances at Henry James's use of the "look" in short fiction. These looks, he says, "send out waves of thought and express, in their special language, deeper meanings than may often be found in stirring action. . . . These meanings are achieved with an art and sensibility that convert the 'mere' look into a major fictional event."[42] But Gargano's own look seems myopic: he calls for more examination of James's use of the look rather than for an exploration of how the look operates with other nonverbal elements.

These fragmented approaches, however, limited as they may be, do confirm the possibilities of new perceptions about familiar works when nonverbal elements are examined. James Joyce's *Dubliners* seems to have been explicated to within inches of its literary life. But Jean-Michel Rabate revives significant interpretation in his "Silence in *Dubliners*." He suggests that Joyce plays games with his readers, using the multiple meanings of silence. "Silence can mean the inversion of speech . . .; silence can reveal . . . a blank space in the text, . . . [where] characters . . . betray themselves by slips, lapsus, omissions; . . . silence being the void element. . . . Silence can finally appear as the end, the limit, the death of speech, its paralysis."[43] As Rabate points out, Stephen's weapons against paralysis--the triad of silence, exile, and cunning--have received uneven attention. Silence permeates *Dubliners*; ultimately "it defines the vanishing point of all assertion, exhibits the empty space which the writing of the text constantly re-covers and recovers, in its multiplication."[44]

Approaching *Dubliners* through silence not only provides new understanding of the stories (especially a complex story such as "The Dead"), but also enables readers to explore Joyce's process of setting "up the possibility of an ethical discourse criticising the paralysis of Dublin"[45] then leaving that possibility behind in the silence of the final story. Furthermore, his approach allows Rabate to show connections among Joyce's works--silent connections.

Certainly Joyce's works would be suitable subjects for a much more comprehensive nonverbal approach. Silence does not operate in isolation from body clues, time, and space, for example. To illustrate a comprehensive nonverbal approach, however, the short fiction of Nathaniel Hawthorne, Ernest Hemingway, and Flannery O'Connor has been chosen. These three authors represent an ideal historical span spaced as they are through 125 years; they represent a geographical diversity; and they represent a technical mastery of the short story form. Why three American authors? Three because each emphasizes different elements of the nonverbal. American because of the importance of limiting such a study to one culture (even though subcultures exist within America), since the decoding of nonverbal elements varies from culture to culture. Such an approach seeks to highlight and not to isolate the role of the nonverbal in fiction. By establishing a field whose confines are the three classifications (regulators, body clues, adaptors) and six codes (physical appearance, vocal tones, touch, space, time, and artifacts), this approach seeks to avoid being entwined in a jungle of jargon and being bogged down by the swamp of singularity.

At times, such an approach offers a significant rereading of the stories discussed. Sometimes, such an approach offers a corrective reading for some previous misreadings of the stories. Always, such an approach adds a dimension. For as Burke suggests, "No work can come to life as an artistic medium unless we, by our modes of interpretation . . . endow its *positions* and *motions* with the quality of *action*. . . . Codes of literary or music notation do not . . . directly appeal. Rather, they are but *instructions* for performing."[45] We must be able to follow these instructions, implicit though they may be, because the ability to decode the nonverbal codes enhances the essential collaboration of the writer and reader of the short story.

Notes

[1] R.P. Blackmur, *Language As Gesture: Essays in Poetry* (London: George Allen and Unwin, 1954), p. 7.

[2] Blackmur paraphrasing a Nijinski remark, p. 9.

[3] Blackmur, p. 8.

[4] Blackmur, p. 7.

[5] Blackmur, p. 11.

[6] Blackmur, p. 20.

[7] Blackmur, p. 13.

[8] Blackmur, p. 17.

[9] *Othello*. iv. ii. 31-32.

[10] See Jonathon Miller, "Plays and Players," in *Non-verbal Communication*, ed. R.A. Hinde (Cambridge: Cambridge Univ. Pres, 1972), pp. 359-73. See also Keir Elam, *The Semiotics of Theatre and Drama* (New York: Methuen, 1980) for a discussion of signs and codes in drama.

[11] Macdonald Critchley, *The Language of Gesture* (London: Folcroft-Edward Arnold, 1970), p. 110.

[12] Huston Diehl, "Inversion, Parody, and Irony: The Visual Rhetoric of Renaissance English Tragedy," *Studies in English Literature*, 22 (Spring 1982), 200.

[13] See Diehl, p. 208.

[14] See stage directions towards the end of scene 5 of Tom Stoppard's, *Professional Foul* in *Every Good Boy Deserves Favor and Professional Foul* (New York: Grove Press, 1978), p. 74.

[15] Stoppard, scene 5, p. 74.

[16] Stoppard, scene 5, p. 75.

[17] Paul A. Eschholz, "Mark Twain and the Language of Gesture," *Mark Twain Journal*, 17 (1973), 5-8.

[18] Mark Twain, *A Connecticut Yankee in King Arthur's Court* (New York: The New American Library, 1963), p. 306.

[19] Mark Twain, *Adventures of Huckleberry Finn* (New York: Harper and Bros., 1923), pp. 67-68.

[20] Eschholz, p. 6.

[21] Eschholz, p. 8.

[22] Frances Freeman Paden, "Autistic Gestures in *The Heart Is a Lonely Hunter*," *Modern Fiction Studies*, 28 (Autumn 1982), 454.

[23] Norman Friedman, "What Makes A Short Story Short?" *Modern Fiction Studies*, 4 (1968), 349-54; rpt.in *Short Story Theories*, p. 130.

[24] Friedman, p. 132.

[25] Charles E. May, "Introduction: A Survey of Short Story Criticism in America," in *Short Story Theories*, p. 5.

[26] Friedman, p. 131.

[27] Ruth Engelken, "Writing with Description," in *Handbook of Short Story Writing*, ed. Frank A. Dickson and Sandra Smythe (Cincinnati: Writers Digest, 1970), p. 75.

[28] Eudora Welty, "The Reading and Writing of Short Stories," *The Atlantic Monthly*, 183 (February 1949), 54-58 and 46-49; rpt. in *Short Story Theories*, p. 172. Welty is commenting on Virginia Woolf's combination of the intellect and the senses in her writing.

[29] Gullason, p. 23.

[30] This phrase is the title of Nadine Gordimer's essay in *Short Story Theories*, pp. 178-81. The essay was originally titled "South Africa" in *Kenyon Review*, 30 (1968), 457-61.

[31] The title of Robert Portune's essay in *Handbook of Short Story Writing*, pp. 66-70.

[32] H.E. Bates, "The Modern Short Story: Retrospect," in *The Modern Short Story: A Critical Survey* (1941; rpt. Boston: The Writer, 1972); rpt. in *Short Story Theories*, p. 77.

[33] Bates, pp. 77-78.

[34] Bates, p. 78.

[35] As paraphrased by Bates, p. 76.

[36] Gullason, pp. 30-31.

[37] James Hilton, "Creating a 'Lovable Character,'" in *Handbook of Short Story Writing*, pp. 56-57.

[38] Bates, p. 77.

[39] See Clayton C. Barbeau, "The Value of a Wart," *Handbook of Short Story Writing*, pp. 51-54.

[40] L.A.G. Strong, "The Story: Notes at Random," *Lovat Dickson's Magazine*, 2 (1934), 281-82 as quoted by A.L. Bader in "The Structure of the

Modern Short Story," *College English*, 7 (1945), 86-92; rpt. in *Short Story Theories*, p. 110.

[41] See Rust Hills, *Writing in General and the Short Story in Particular: An Informal Textbook* (Boston: Houghton Mifflin, 1977), pp. 76-79.

[42] James W. Gargano, "The 'Look' as a Major Event in James's Short Fiction," *Arizona Quarterly*, 43 (1979), 320.

[43] Jean-Michel Rabate, "Silence in *Dubliners*," in *James Joyce: New Perspectives*, ed. Colin McCabe (Brighton: Indiana Univ. Press, 1982), p. 45.

[44] Rabate, p. 68.

[45] As quoted in Chester Clayton Long, *The Liberal Art of Interpretation* (New York: Harper and Row, 1974), p. 15.

Chapter 3
NOISY NATHANIEL

"May not one man have several voices?. . . ."

Gentleman in "My Kinsman, Major
Molineux."

Hawthorne makes demands of his readers. The deliberate ambiguity he frequently employs--especially at the end of stories--requires the collaboration of sensitive readers. For Hawthorne does provide clues. Despite all the attention to Hawthorne's life, mind, and art, many of the nonverbal elements in his work have gone largely unremarked. This neglect is regrettable because the application of a systematic nonverbal reading to many of his stories provides answers to the questions posed by fictional performances that are bathed in ambiguity.

It is also surprising because Hawthorne literally shouts out his consciousness of the nonverbal in his best work; there may never have been such a noisy writer as Nathaniel Hawthorne. Although vocal tones represent the dominant nonverbal code employed by Hawthorne in creating the special atmosphere that permeates his stories, he also makes varying use of the other nonverbal techniques. Many have commented on his special atmosphere; most have attributed it to Hawthorne's masterful manipulation of moonlit scenes, to his precise presentation of "the symbol, the historical past, the allegorical framework of myth, and the multiple perspective."[1] This is all true. But at times, many critics seem too readily lured into Hawthorne's "intermediate space"[2] of "The Haunted Mind"--that space somewhere between sleep and waking--and too easily diverted from surface realities by the temptation to seek Hawthorne's inner truth beyond the story itself. As Mary Rohrberger puts it, Hawthorne believed "that truth lies not in the external facts of appearances but beyond the facts in an inner reality."[3] This, too, is all true. But as Rohrberger herself points out, "The artist creates an illusion of the real. The author manipulates certain facts and uses certain devices to aid the illusion."[4]

It is these "facts" and these "devices" that must be kept in the spotlight even if Hawthorne continually bathes them in moonlight. And a striking number of these facts and devices evolve from Hawthorne's sensitivity to the nonverbal. An examination of these elements in detail in one of Hawthorne's finest stories will not only reveal his dependence on something more than simple dialogue and blatant allegory, but will also show that this method can help solve some of the critical controversies that surround the best of his stories.

Such a story is "My Kinsman, Major Molineux." Having been just about dormant for over a century, this story seemingly erupted into reader and critical attention during the last thirty years. And for good reason. This is arguably Hawthorne's finest story with something for every type of critic to relish; it invites a multitude of approaches, and it has received considerable critical attention. This overflow of criticism, however, does not seem to have exhausted the possibilities inherent in the story. Sometimes critics with radically different approaches praise their colleagues and complement rather than contradict their interpretations. For example, it is not unusual for those offering an historical reading to concede the mythological or initiatory possibilities in the story. Sometimes, however, critics with the same approach vehemently disagree with one another. For instance, the psychoanalytical Louis Paul takes his peers to task. Indeed, he even goes so far as to rewrite a portion of Simon O. Lesser's article for him changing "something which every young man does. . . . [Robin] is destroying an image of paternal authority"[5] to "something which every *neurotic* young man does . . . *not* destroying *but unconsciously preserving* an image of paternal authority."[6] And sometimes critics reject an overall approach outright. Roy Harvey Pearce, for example, laments that all the psychoanalytical critics seem to divorce Robin from the rest of the story; Pearce pleads with these critics to redress their sins "by taking Robin off the couch and putting him back into the tale."[7]

Whether on the couch or in the tale, though, Robin poses most problems for the critics by his comments and behavior at the end of the story. This typically ambiguous Hawthornian ending prompts Edwin Haviland Miller to term it a "deliberately inconclusive conclusion."[8] Yet definite opinions exist about its meaning, with the majority viewing the ending as being a positive one. Frederick C. Crews, along with several notable allies, feels that the finale shows Robin "has cathartically rid himself of both filial dependence and filial resentment, and will now be free, as his benevolent friend expects, to 'rise in the world without the help of your kinsman, Major Molineux.'"[9] Nonsense, suggests Miller, who is diametrically opposed to this viewpoint; he argues that "part of Hawthorne is too much a psychic realist, too skeptical, to have faith in catharses or metamorphoses. . . ."[10] Between these two poles stands Paul, who diagnoses Robin's psyche as having remained basically unchanged because "his unconscious longing for submission to an idealized father still persists."[11] Richard Harter Fogle cannot be that conclusive about Robin: "Left with this reversal of his expectations, at the end of the story he has presumably learned his lesson."[12] Hawthorne himself would have approved Fogle's tentative vocabulary--the elusiveness of Fogle's "presumably" rivaling his own "perhaps" (11, 231).

Hawthorne's elusiveness at the end of the story cannot be denied. But along the way he has littered the streets of Boston with clues--many of them nonverbal. Occasionally, critics have drawn attention to one nonverbal aspect or another in passing, but no extensive attention has been given to either the range or depth of Hawthorne's aptitude for the nonverbal. "My Kinsman, Major Molineux" represents Hawthorne's most concerted and creative use of his favorite nonverbal code: vocal tones. Many critics have noticed and commented on one aspect of vocal tones: the laughter that resonates and reverberates throughout this story--and throughout much of Hawthorne's work.

As Robert Dusenbery points out in "Hawthorne's Merry Company: The Anatomy of Laughter in the Tales and Short Stories," Hawthorne's *American Notebooks* reveal his fascination with laughter.[13] Rarely in Hawthorne, though, does laughter echo spontaneous joy. Indeed, Hawthorne suggests in "Ethan Brand" just how discordant a note laughter can strike:

> Laughter, when out of place, mistimed, or bursting forth
> from a disordered state of feeling, may be the most
> terrible modulation of the human voice. The laughter of
> one asleep, even if it be a little child,--the madman's
> laugh,--the wild screaming laugh of a born idiot, are
> sounds that we sometimes tremble to hear, and would always
> willingly forget. Poets have imagined no utterance of
> fiends or hobgoblins so fearfully inappropriate as a laugh
> (11, 87-88).

Apart from its sinister qualities, what else attracted Hawthorne to laughter? Ambiguity. Although character after character laughs in "My Kinsman, Major Molineux," no two characters laugh alike or for the same apparent reason. From the barber's shop comes "an ill-mannered roar" (11, 211); from the inn "a general laugh" rings out, "in which the innkeeper's voice might be distinguished, like the dropping of small stones into a kettle" (11,217).

"Along the solitary street," Robin hears "the sound of drowsy laughter" (11, 218) and "the pleasant titter" (11, 218) of the scarlet lady. As the night turns nightmarish, Robin hears, among a blast of sounds, "a wild and confused laughter" (11, 226) which increases in volume and mixes with the "shrill voices of mirth and terror" (11, 228) of several women running along the sidewalk. And then, as if echoing and underscoring the laughter he has already heard, Robin is treated to a chorus, a medley of perverted merriment:

> At that moment a voice of sluggish merriment saluted Robin's ears; he turned instinctively, and just behind the corner of the church stood the lantern-bearer. . . . Then he heard a peal of laughter like the ringing of silvery bells; a woman twitched his arm, a saucy eye met his, and he saw the lady of the scarlet petticoat. A sharp dry cachinnation appealed to his memory, and he beheld the courteous little innkeeper. And lastly, there sailed over the heads of the multitude a great, broad laugh, broken in the midst by two sepulchral hems. . . . The old citizen . . . . Supported himself on his polished cane in a fit of convulsive merriment, which manifested itself on his solemn old features like a funny inscription on a tombstone. Then Robin seemed to hear the voices of the barbers, of the guests of the inn, and of all who had made sport of him that night (11, 229-30).

The object of all this "frenzied merriment" (11, 230)? Major Molineux in all his "tar-and-feathery dignity" (11, 228). Robin responds, too, with a climactic burst:

> The contagion was spreading among the multitude, when, all at once, it seized upon Robin, and he sent forth a shout

of laughter that echoed through the street; every man shook his sides, every man emptied his lungs, but Robin's shout was the loudest there (11, 230).

This particular laugh and general laughter in Hawthorne cause critics considerable consternation and confusion. Franklin B. Newman at first complains that Hawthorne disappoints readers because the tone of this laugh needs clarification; Newman's own disappointment, however, doesn't last long, as he soon, almost confidently, asserts that Robin "laughs in a sense of outrage, partly at himself, partly at the Major, and considerably at the state of human nature."[14] Fogle concurs:

The laughter in "My Kinsman, Major Molineux" commences as discord and apparently cruel mockery, but expands until it becomes cosmic, impersonal, an exquisite light-hearted critique of man himself. . . . The cruelty of it does not wholly vanish, but is sublimated and spiritualized. Robin, caught up with it, laughs at himself and inevitably at his poor kinsman. Undergoing a reaction that is both emotional and intellectual, he is shaken, purged, emptied, and cleansed.[15]

Others refuse to hear that much assertiveness in the laugh. Daniel Hoffman, for instance, suggests that "not even the shame, the agony of his Kinsman, not even his own emotions of pity and terror, can hold him from making 'their frenzied merriment' his own. There are buffetings of passion, there are possibilities of evil and of guilt, which Robin's callow rationalism cannot fathom."[16] Robin's laugh may have been the loudest, but it does not seem to have been the clearest.

When talking about laughter in all of Hawthorne, however, the critics more closely agree. Dusenbery believes laughter in Hawthorne has several functions: it moves the plot; it "foreshadows gloom or records merely the hollow mind or the corrupt soul turning upon itself in mockery"; and, most importantly for any consideration of its nonverbal implications, it "is used as a dramatic device for revealing character."[17] In the other major article on this subject, "Smiles and Laughter in Hawthorne," Mary Allen agrees that Hawthorne uses laughter to reveal character; she cites as an example Chillingworth in *The Scarlet Letter*, whose attempts to lie with his face support what the nonverbal research contends frequently occurs with facial lies: failure. "Chillingworth's hypocritical smile makes an unsuccessful facade: it is his wish and purpose to mask a fierce and guarded expression with a smile, 'but the latter played him false, and flickered over his visage so derisively, that the spectator could see his blackness all the better for it.'"[18] Then Allen takes two further steps. The first is down the fascinating but dangerous path of psychobiographic analysis; she hypothesizes that Hawthorne's use of laughter shows that he fears pleasure. The second is down the surer but not much clearer path of analysis; she concludes:

> In the dark lives of Hawthorne's people, who so need comic relief, there is none. Rather than reflecting light and happy hearts, their smiles and laughter reveal the weight of experience, sin, and hypocrisy. The signs of mirth may clearly indicate corruption, but they may show, brilliantly, the often indecipherable nature of good and evil forces.[19]

And where does that leave the reader? "More baffled and disturbed than before."[20] Ambiguity. Hawthorne would have been pleased. For had Hawthorne been writing today, he could hardly have picked a nonverbal mode of expression more mystifying than laughter. Indeed, Allen's "baffled" is echoed by J. A. R. A. M. Van Hooff in one of the most extensive articles on laughter and smiling in the literature on the nonverbal; he writes that many researchers remain "baffled" by how spontaneous and automatic laughter seems on the one hand, "and the subtle spirituality of the stimuli that can release it on the other. . . ."[21] Van Hooff's observations on laughter, based on a review of the literature of laughter, on studies of children's laughter, and on studies of comparable signs in primates, do offer some possible insights into laughs in "My Kinsman, Major Molineux." Van Hooff points out that one controversial school of thought, including Freud, sees laughter as a release of tension with primitive origins. When danger passes laughter signals relaxation; and if the passing of the danger includes the capturing of a foe, then laughter has the dual function of "the savage shout of triumph and the cruel mockery over a conquered enemy."[22] The word "shout" may be a key one, for Hawthorne uses that same word not once, but twice in a sentence that describes Robin laughing. And apparently everyone in the crowd shouted out laughter. Triumph and mockery? Yes.

The triumph of the crowd comes from the symbolic rejection of an alien political object--in this instance, the seemingly honorable Major Molineux. Hawthorne has carefully crafted the historical rather than the personal basis for this rejection in the very first paragraph of the story. The unfortunate colonial governors, Hawthorne tells us, were targets of hostility from the colonists and "the reprehension" (11, 208) of their superiors in England for "softening their instructions" (11, 208). This opening paragraph has presented almost as many difficulties as the concluding paragraph. Why would Hawthorne seem so unsympathetic to the colonists? As Miller puts it, the story "presents the Colonists as a secretive, vindictive, perhaps sadistic mob and would seem to say, if it makes a political statement, that for English tyranny is substituted the tyranny of a democratic mob."[23] Roger P. Wallins accounts for this opening by suggesting that a narrator rather than Hawthorne is giving this history lesson and this "is a technique to convince the reader that the narrator is sufficiently fair-minded . . . to examine an idea unpopular with his audience."[24] Wallins may be correct. But few readers, by his own admission, spot the technique. Whatever Hawthorne's intentions, he does provide a continuity for triumph: at least six previous governors had suffered ignominy—and sometimes worse—[25] at the hands of the colonists.

Major Molineux's tarred-and-feathered ride represents a painful public rejection of what he represents: the crown. Ambiguity again. Part of the mob had been quite happy earlier the same evening to drink in an inn decorated with the sign "of a British hero" (11, 212). This is only one of several disorienting features facing Robin. As Miller points out, "innocent behavior is threatened with jail and the stocks; a venerable old man acts like a churl, while a prostitute speaks with exemplary civility."[26] Yet all disparate elements—and all disparate laughs—merge to mock. Although no conclusive research has been conducted on the aggressive motivation of laughter, R. J. Andrew predicts that such research will reveal that "laughter is usual only when the human who is mocked is being treated as an object to be viewed . . . and that laughter disappears when attacks (e.g. pushes, kicks, stone-throwing) develop."[27] This would seem to fit the scene. Actual physical hostility has preceded the parade of "counterfeited pomp" (11, 230), and now the crowd views and mocks the Major in his open cart for what he represents, not apparently for himself.

Major Molineux, though, receives a more painful personal rejection than his public humiliation: "Perhaps the bitterest pang of all was when his eyes met those of Robin" (11, 229). Something worse follows the penetrating, nonverbal glare: Robin's laugh. Robin does not know the source of this laugh: he becomes intoxicated by "mental inebriety" (11, 229); he becomes "seized" by "the contagion . . . spreading among the multitude" (11, 230).

The laugh may betoken a personal or psychological triumph, as some have suggested. It may represent the mockery of an object (that is, a father figure) which has to be symbolically rejected. In these ways, it parallels the noise of the mob. And perhaps one reason Robin laughs the loudest is that he alone seems to be faced with a totally unexpected, almost ludicrous scene. As Van Hooff explains, many researchers concentrating on the releasing factors in laughter put "the emphasis on some contrast, unexpected change or contradiction in the situation."[28] The mob expects and has been preparing all evening for this events; Robin neither expects it nor, because of his inability to detect the clues, has he been prepared for it. All these factors combine to unleash his laugh--a laugh which has to remain, no doubt as Hawthorne intended, ambiguous.

Hawthorne's use of laughter may be as deceiving as a hyena's. For it tends, through its dominance, to diminish the volume of his other, more subtle, yet much less ambiguous, use of vocal tones. These tones reverberate with meaning. But first they must be heard by readers. For Robin's journey can be mapped with great assurance through listening to his tones of voice and through noting the tones of those who speak to him. Almost without exception, Hawthorne describes the tones of his characters adjectivally or adverbally, and these tones frequently reveal more than the words themselves. Like his laughter, Robin's first speech--suitably a question--"was uttered very loudly" (11, 211). Hiding behind his loudness and holding onto the old man's coat, Robin receives instant hostility and chilling mystery from his first urban reply: "The citizen . . . answered him in a tone of excessive anger and annoyance. His two sepulchral hems, however, broke into the very centre of his rebuke, with most singular effect, like a thought of the cold grave obtruding among wrathful passions" (11, 211). Is this to be the voice of the town?

Like the laughs, the voices of the town have various tones but a combined effect. Thomas E. Connors catalogues the town's tones: "The citizen with the impotent threats, the innkeeper with false accusations, the prostitute with deceit, the watchman with silence, the masquerador with irony, the gentleman with amusement."[29] All these tones conceal the truth and answer the gentleman's question, for a man may indeed "have several voices . . . as well as two complexions" (11, 226). The townspeople probably know what fate is in store for the Major and certainly know what hostility faces his office. They never tell Robin. Only two people aid Robin and then only in obscure ways. The satanic figure tells him Major Molineux will pass by within an hour; the gentleman confirms this: "The Major will very shortly pass through the street" (11, 225). Dennis Brown believes that Robin's seemingly kind guide may be the most damaging of all the townspeople, crueler even than the devilish leader; Brown accuses the guide of being "particularly callous" because "he in no way prepares the young man for his final shock, nor offers him comfort afterwards, but adopts an unfeeling neutrality."[30] How does Robin react to these many voices, to the outright hostility, and to the eventual neutrality? With many voices, outright hostility, and eventual neutrality.

For Robin works hard to earn his self-appointed epithet of "shrewd youth." He does not, however, give himself that name until well into the story--by which time it has become more appropriate than the first five references to shrewdness, which the narrator makes with considerable irony. Take the first use of the term, for example. Following his rude rejection by the old man, Robin searches for a reason, and, the narrator tells us, "being a shrewd youth, soon thought himself able to account for the mystery" (11, 211). His "shrewd" conclusion lacks any factual basis or logical reality:

> "This is some country representative," was his conclusion,
> "who has never seen the inside of my Kinsman's door, and
> lacks the breeding to answer a stranger civilly. The man
> is old, or verily--I might be tempted to turn back and
> smite him on the nose" (11, 211).

Further, it exhibits considerable irony. Shouting his own question was hardly civil; thinking of smiting him on the nose shows the hostility that exists in Robin. This hostility surfaces several times in the story--each time through the manipulation of his oak cudgel. He thinks about "breaking the courteous innkeeper's head" (11, 214); he decides to demand "violently and with lifted cudgel, the necessary guidance" (11, 216). Each time, he decides against using the cudgel--in the first instance because he was outnumbered, in the second instance because he comes upon the scarlet lady. Eventually, though he does use this link with his country past, this thinly veiled symbol of masculinity: he bars the way of a bulky man with his cudgel and responds to the man's threats by "thrusting its larger end close to the man's muffled face" (11, 220). Robin is not quite the complete moral innocent some like to portray.

When he identifies himself as "shrewd" (11, 225), Robin has experienced his dream of home--a dream which by its very nature communicates nonverbally and which the narrator specifically refers to as Robin's thoughts that "become visible and audible" (11, 233):

> He perceived the slight inequality of his father's voice
> when he came to speak of the Absent One: he noted how his
> Mother turned her face to the broad and knotted trunk; how
> his elder brother scorned . . . to permit his features to
> be moved; how his younger sister drew down a low hanging
> ranch before her eyes; and how the little one . . . burst
> into clamorous grief (11, 223).

The vocal tones of father and child and the body clues of mother, brother, and sister are all imagined--perhaps accurately so, but certainly as a reflection of what has so disillusioned Robin in the city: the lack of regard from all for his family ties. Robin at this stage desperately wants to feel missed. But he doesn't go home--not even in his dream; he wakes up and soon announces his shrewdness. And with some justification, for each scene shows a little growth--witness his ability to distinguish between the nonverbal truth and the verbal lies of the prostitute. In a series of body clues which truly display, the prostitute gives Robin the eye: "The occasional sparkle of an eye, as if the moonbeams were trembling on some bright thing" (11, 216); "The sparkle of a saucy eye" (11, 219). Robin reads her eyes and sees through her alluring voice. "Even though the airy counterpart of a stream of melted silver, . . . he could not help doubting whether that sweet voice spoke Gospel truth" (11, 217). Robin's shrewdness, though, does not save him; a watchman with "a long staff, spiked at the end" (11, 218) does. For the nonverbal touch of the lady of the night proves stronger than her words or than the brawny Robin--he had been, "half-willing" (11, 218), on his way in when the watchman surfaces. He had been shrewd enough to "read in her eyes when he did not hear in her words" (11, 218), but, as when he laughs, Robin seems immersed in this new and not altogether unwelcome atmosphere. Once the spell is broken, however,--and perhaps it's no coincidence that Hawthorne links the watchman, through his lantern "like the moonshine of Pyramus and Thisbe" (11, 218), to the magical *A Midsummer Night's Dream*[31]--Robin can resist the second temptation.

Neither the narrator nor Robin can quite convince the reader that the young man fully deserves the title of shrewdness. Certainly Robin learns some things quickly. He soon catches on to the terms of law-and-order in the town. Threatened by the watchman with being placed in the stocks for dallying with the prostitute, Robin remembers not only the punishment, but also the exact words of the watchman when he himself responds to the sounds of riotous behavior: the watch will "set them in the stocks by peep of day" (11, 226). By the end of the story, some growth is evident. Wallins makes a convincing case that the first time a character calls Robin "shrewd" is the first time the word has no ironic overtones. This occurs in the last sentence when the gentleman tells Robin: "Or, if you prefer to remain with us, perhaps, as you are a shrewd youth, you may rise in the world, without the help of your Kinsman, Major Molineux" (11, 231). Wallins concludes: "By the end of the story, then, we receive an objective corroboration of the beginning growth we had observed earlier."[32] The several voices of Robin throughout, and the nonverbal clues at the end, support Wallins' reading rather than those readings which suggest no growth in Robin.

Robin's tones begin in protective loudness, moderate to fragile confidence, and move into ironic cunning. After he ceases to understand voices and after he seems destined to fail in his supposed quest, his tones reveal a greater grasp of reality even as they become more desperate and less confident. His final tone--coupled with his facial display--suggests that he has indeed grown to the point of being able to modulate his voice to a tone that echoes with the loss of innocence. Initially, though, his loudness sounds like naivete. So, too, do his tones to the innkeeper, whose own voice was never known "to change . . . from the one shrill note in which he now addressed Robin" (11, 213). Robin exhibits a confidence based more on his expectations than on reality. He begins his response to the innkeeper "with such an assumption of consequence, as befitted the Major's relative" (11, 213); he changes his tone in midsentence by "lowering his voice" (11, 213); and he concludes "with lofty confidence" (11, 213). Ironically, then, Robin is the first character in the story to display "several voices." It is contagious. After Robin's confidence has been shown to be misplaced--through his total misinterpretation of the hostile movement in the room "as expressing the eagerness of each individual to become his guide" (11, 214)--even the innkeeper seems, perhaps for the first time in his life, to change the pitch of his voice. As he pretends to read a wanted poster, the innkeeper breaks "his speech into little dry fragments" (11, 214). Robin understands; he leaves.

In his next major encounter, Robin again shows the variety of his voice--this time to the fair lady in the scarlet petticoat. Wanting an answer to his question, Robin has little difficulty in speaking in a "plaintive and winning" (11, 217) voice. He almost wins more than he bargains for. Her "sweet voice" (11, 217) utters an alluring lie: "Major Molineux dwells here" (11, 217). But Robin at least understands the basics of artifacts--in this instance, the environs and architecture:

> He looked up and down the mean street, and then surveyed
> the house before which they stood. It was a small, dark
> edifice of two stories, the second of which projected over
> the lower floor; and the front apartment had the aspect of
> a shop for petty commodities (11, 217).

Since Robin cannot connect this brothel to the Major's mansion (which, despite all his wanderings, he never finds), he replies "cunningly" (11, 217). All his cunning, though, quickly disintegrates under her light touch; once again, the tone of his voice has not quite matched the tone of his behavior. Before he can lose his innocence, however, Robin is spared; Hawthorne wants to save Robin for a more crushing initiation. Enter the watchman--with a yawn and with a voice that hardly seems likely to scare, as his "accents . . . seemed to fall asleep as soon as they were uttered" (11, 218). The threat of the stocks is almost enough, however. Robin reverts to one last loud question "shouted lustily" (11, 218) at the watchman. The silence that follows is almost as loud. And when the saucy lady seeks him out again, Robin's lustiness has been expended. Robin understands; he leaves.

What Robin does not understand are the words soon addressed to him by two bands of men "in outlandish attire" (11, 219): "They did but utter a few words in some language of which Robin knew nothing" (11, 219). For the first time in the story, Robin is struck speechless. And then he is struck by hostile words: "perceiving his inability to answer, [they] bestowed a curse upon him in plain English . . ." (11, 219). This ambiguous encounter undermines Robin's vocal confidence and cunning; no longer will he hide behind inappropriate tones. Although largely ignored by the critics, this paragraph is a crucial one. Robin has, also for the first time, begun to roam "desperately, and at random" (11, 219); he has lost his fragile faith in himself to the extent that he is "almost ready to believe that a spell was on him" (11, 219). The setting provides no solace, either. The surface warmth of the inn and the seductions of the brothel are behind him. So, too, is the "spacious street . . . with lofty houses . . . and the lamps . . . [in] numerous shop windows" (11, 215). Now "the streets lay before him, strange and desolate, and the lights were extinguished in almost every house" (11, 219). Previously, a church had rung its bells in a reassuring sound (11, 215). Now another church merely casts a "shade" (11, 219) which partially hides and disguises the same threatening character he had eluded in the previous street scene.

Robin's voice now utters a question "very resolutely" (11, 219). Like all his voices from this point on, his tone reflects truthfulness--as his actions confirm: "Robin planted himself full before him" (11, 219). Resolute Robin[33] doesn't run even when faced with a threat far more hostile than either the inkeeper's or the watchman's: "'Keep your tongue between your teeth, fool, and let me pass,' said a deep, gruff voice, which Robin partly remembered. 'Let me pass, I say, or I'll strike you to the earth!'" (11, 220). Robin "cried" (11, 220) out another resolute response; he cannot be cowed by words alone anymore. Yet body clues and physical appearances combine to challenge him further. First "the stranger . . . unmuffled his own face and stared full into that of Robin" (11, 220). Such a stare alone can be disquieting; studies on staring and gaze suggest that these body clues can signal dominance, threats, and hostility.[34] The same person shakes Robin with a stare during the parade, causing him to speak in a discomfited tone which equates with the state of his psyche:

> "The double-faced fellow has his eye upon me," muttered
> Robin, with an indefinite but uncomfortable idea, that he
> was himself to bear a part in the pageantry (11, 228).

But the previous times that this man penetrates Robin with his stare, he also shocks him with his physical appearance. Early in the story, Robin notices this man in the inn with his grotesque features:

> The forehead bulged out into a double prominence, with a
> vale between; the nose came boldly forth in an irregular
> curve, and its bridge was of more than a finger's breadth;
> the eyebrows were deep and shaggy, and the eyes glowed
> beneath them like fire in a cave (11, 213).

As he leaves the inn, "he encountered a sneering glance from the bold-featured personage . . . "(11, 214). In the confrontation scene, Robin notices a change in the features, a terrifying change: "One side of the face blazed of an intense red, while the other was black as midnight" (11, 220). Finally, in this middle scene, the man leaves--but not without a final disquieting facial display: "The stranger grinned in Robin's face" (11, 220).

Robin responds in a passionate tone with a comment where Hawthorne's verb to describe the tone creates a greater impression than the words themselves: "'Strange things we travellers see!' ejaculated Robin" (11, 220). His passion quickly becomes expended, and he waits for his kinsman to appear rather than travelling further to find him. He waits; he listens. And he hears "a murmur . . . a low, dull, dreamy sound, compounded of many noises" (11, 221), which he mistakes for the "snore of a sleeping town" (11, 221). And he hears periodic shouts, at which he "marvelled" (11, 221). These "sleep-inspiring" (11, 221) sounds combine with the disquieting environment of the church interior, and Robin's heart shivers "with a sensation of loneliness" (11, 222). He dreams of home; he wakes when in his dream the door "latch tinkled into its place, and he was excluded from his home" (11, 223). The dream disturbs and confuses Robin further: "Am I here, or there?' cried Robin, starting" (11, 223). Again his tone--"cried"--confirms this mental state.

His mental state soon turns from disturbed to desperate as "his mind kept vibrating between fancy and reality" (11, 223). Hallucinations, artifacts, nature, and humanity become interchangeable in his muddled mind: "The pillars of the balcony lengthened into the tall, bare stems of pines, dwindled down to human figures, settled again in their true shape and size, and then commenced a new succession of changes" (11, 223). J. C. Nitzsche would have us believe that "the identification of the pillars with pine trees--civilization with nature--suggests a prelapsarian vision of the world as a place where food, clothing, and shelter on one level, and fellowship, charity, and love on a higher level, appear naturally, abundantly, openly, as in Eden."[35] It seems more likely, however, that Hawthorne wants to convey Robin's inability to grasp reality--an inability which frustrates Robin and which causes his next statement to be couched "in a loud, peevish, and lamentable cry" (11, 224). Robin may still be loud (now from frustration rather than pretended confidence), but Hawthorne accentuates Robin's progressive psychological disintegration by describing a tone three ways for the first time in the story. And although Robin's voice continues to reveal distress, he never again sinks to such depths, and Hawthorne never again compounds his adjectives to describe a tone.

What brings this slight relief to Robin? A tone of voice, naturally. The gentleman Robin has addressed so desperately responds "in a tone of real kindness, which had become strange to Robin's ears" (11, 224). Even though Robin replies to this kindness "despondingly" (11, 224), Hawthorne makes his descriptions of tones less desperate, more neutral as the dialogue continues: "related" (11, 224), "observed" (11, 224), "continued" (11, 225), "replied" (11, 225), "inquired" (11, 225), "asked" (11, 226), "interrupted" (11, 226), "responded" (11, 226), "exclaimed" (11, 226), and "answered" (11, 227). Brown correctly points out that the substance of this dialogue is of little value to Robin, but he has not listened closely enough to the tones of both the gentleman and Robin. The very neutrality that Brown calls "unfeeling," the very man Brown calls "callous" are both essential in preparing Robin for the climax. Through the course of the dialogue, Robin--as revealed by his tones-- has managed to gain some stability even as the noise and confusion around him approach a crescendo. Certainly his response to meeting Major Molineux incorporates all of the evening's events and the contagion of the mob. More importantly, it reveals the response of a young man who has survived the preceding trials and who has arrived at his most level psychological state just prior to the Major's arrival. This helps account for his ability to learn from the painful climax.

Robin reveals this change through his actions, his face, and his voice in the concluding section of the story. The gentleman continues his nonverbal reassurance by "laying his hand on the youth's shoulder" (11, 230) as he poses a question which receives no verbal answer: "Well, Robin, are you dreaming?" (11, 230). Robin releases his hold on "the stone post, to which he had instinctively clung" (11, 230). He has not been drowned by "the living stream" (11, 230) of humanity, but he has been able to get his feet wet in adult urban society. And such initiation has a cost--the cost of adolescent rural innocence. This cost, this loss shows on his face: "His cheek was somewhat pale, and his eye not quite so lively as in the earlier part of the evening" (11, 230). Robin at last speaks in a tone of adulthood. Gone are the juvenile tones ("plaintive," "peevish," for example). Gone are the neutral tones ("related," "observed," for example). Present is a tone which requires a level of sophistication and a measure of cynicism: "dryly" (11, 230). He has abandoned his sticks (oak cudgel) and stones (the post) and armed his words with a cutting edge. His shrewdness and his knowledge, of course, remain incomplete, for he is still a youth. Seeing the town in daylight rather than in the moonlight which "gave something of romance to a scene, that might not have possessed it in the light of day" (11, 221) will be the next step in the enlightening of Robin Molineux.

When he does see the town by daylight, Robin will undoubtedly get a clearer picture--visually and psychologically. He will, for example, probably be able to assimilate many of the artifacts which overpower him by night. As Burgoon and Saine have pointed out, artifacts appeal to the senses; the senses, however, are capable of being overloaded, quickly leading to weariness--the very word Hawthorne uses in describing "that evening of ambiguity and weariness" (11, 222). Naturally, noise (a nonverbal code which, in addition to its role in vocal tones, plays an important role in artifacts) has made the largest single contribution to this condition. But other aspects of artifacts play a role in the story--particularly the often symbolic architecture.

Nitzsche, in his comprehensive study of "House Symbolism in Hawthorne's 'My Kinsman, Major Molineux,'" suggests that "the houses that Robin visits in the tale exemplify phases in his progress toward understanding the true nature of the house or home. . . ."[36] Certainly houses give Robin problems, as do the streets themselves. He cannot find what must be the most prominent home in the most desirous neighborhood--the elusive governor's mansion. He cannot comprehend the appearance of a brothel. He cannot distinguish the pillars of the mansion from pine trees. He cannot rest in the inn nor at the church. When he tries to absorb the overall architecture, he "began to grow wearisome" (11, 221).

Whereas the specific architecture influences Robin's psyche, the streets and general architecture reflect his changing psyche. Again Hawthorne's use of artifacts exactly parallels what nonverbal research shows: the power of artifacts to influence behavior and to reflect power and status.

As Robin airily steps into town like the American version of Dick Whittington ("as if he were entering London city" [11, 210]), he believes he bears power and status from his affinity with his important kinsman. But as soon as he realizes that he doesn't know where to go, his vision of the immediate scene reflects his general inadequacy and the current qualities of his psyche: "the narrow street . . . the small and mean wooden buildings . . . scattered on either side" (11, 210). However, once he devises a plan of action (to pay the next person he meets a shilling to tell him the way), the streets and his mind momentarily broaden: "the street now became wider, and the houses more respectable in their appearance" (11, 210). Just as his tones of voice reveal his initial insecurity and his immediate vulnerability to psychological reversals, so does the cartography of the town. The wide streets and respectable houses soon disappear after his abrasive encounter with the old man: "He now became entangled in a succession of crooked and narrow streets, which crossed each other, and meandered . . . The streets were empty, the shops were closed, and lights were visible only in the second stories of a few dwelling-houses" (11, 211-12). His mind becomes more entangled than his legs.

Nor does a visit to a tavern hold much promise for peace of mind. Its interior—size, arrangement, lighting, colors, and sounds—and its inhabitants—drunken mariners and laborers, sheepish countrymen, a peevish innkeeper, and a grotesque stranger—do nothing to help Robin. The tavern "was a long and low apartment, with oaken walls, grown dark in the continual smoke, and a floor, which was thickly sanded, but of no immaculate purity" (11, 212); it had dark corners; it stood in a "narrow lane" (11, 215). The customers and the innkeeper react to Robin darkly; Robin is too narrow in vision to see through the dark walls initially. So he suffers another demoralizing reversal. Instead of receiving the anticipated directions to his kinsman's house, he flinches from the innkeeper's oblique threat and the blatant threat on the face of the crowd: "a strange hostility in every countenance, induced him to relinquish his purpose of breaking the courteous innkeeper's head" (11, 214).

Even when Robin finds a more inviting area of town, it is no less mystifying and no more able to embrace him. The "spacious street," the "lofty houses," and the brightly dressed and humming "imitators of the European fine gentlemen of the period" (11, 215) merely make Robin feel inadequate. The jaunty, "half-dancing" gait of the pedestrians leaves "poor Robin ashamed of his quiet and natural gait" (11, 215). He tries to find his way out of the maze of his own mind by staring at people; they, not surprisingly, react with hostility: Robin suffers "some rebukes from the impertinence of his scrutiny into people's faces" (11, 215). When he tries his luck on the other side of the street, he hears the approach of the man with two sepulchral hems; Robin leaves the street. And consistent with the oscillation between types of architecture throughout the story, Hawthorne next places Robin in the lowest and "reddest" district of town. From the brothel, Robin then moves to the church. No wonder the youth is confused.

Eventually, however, he stops wandering--although not wondering. Once Robin sits on the steps near the church, he stays there and his mind begins to confuse dream and reality. The kind gentleman prevents him from further physical journeying, realizing that Robin is about to embark on a great psychological journey in the impending encounter with his kinsman. Robin is ready to step round yet another corner by a "darkish house" (11, 226), but the gentleman counsels him to wait. Robin waits. Robin sees. Robin changes. The street he is left in is, for once, simply described as "a silent street" (11, 230). These streets, these houses all have been part of his education and all have added to Robin's earlier confusion and the reader's final understanding. The total environment shows Robin's disorientation far beyond the needs of establishing merely an historical setting. And, as Burgoon and Saine indicate, the overall effect of lighting on the scene can be a crucial factor in the sensory perception of all other aspects of artifacts. With the moonlight and the many lanterns[37] providing the light--in this and many other Hawthorne stories--it is little wonder that Robin cannot see everything.

Hawthorne, however, allows his readers to see a great deal; in particular, he makes substantial use of physical appearance and adornments. Looking at Robin for the first time, for example, the reader and the ferryman see a fine physical specimen with "vigorous shoulders. . . . Brown, curly hair, well-shaped features, and bright, cheerful eyes . . ." (1, 209). This is

a promising description. Robin looks to be strong, resolute, and
lively--qualities not entirely adequate for the experiences ahead but
qualities nonetheless essential to his eventual survival. Even before
Hawthorne describes Robin's physique, however, he describes his clothing:

> He was clad in a coarse grey coat, well worn, but in
> excellent repair, his under garments were durably
> constructed of leather, and tight to a pair of serviceable
> and well-shaped limbs; his stockings of blue yarn were the
> incontrovertible handiwork of a mother or a sister; and on
> his head was a three-cornered hat, which in its better
> days had perhaps sheltered the graver brow of the lad's
> father (11, 209).

His clothes reveal not only that he was "evidently country-bred" (11, 209),
but also that he was a member of a closeknit rural family which took a
communal interest in his dress. Since the role of family (leaving and longing
for one branch of kin, searching for and rejecting another) plays an important
role in the story ("My Kinsman, . . ."), this early link to family provides
readers with a hook on which to hang those carefully described clothes. And
in case readers miss this early point, Hawthorne provides two mirrors. First,
he repeats the description of Robin when the young man arrives at the tavern.
Second, he allows Robin to stress the familial and sartorial connection just
before the climactic scene: "So my mother and sister put me in handsome trim"
(11, 225).

The clothes of the first person whom Robin meets in the town underscore
the rural-urban contrast: the man "with a full periwig of grey hair" wore "a
wide-skirted coat of dark cloth, and silk stockings rolled about his knees.
He carried a long and polished cane . . ."(11, 210). Dressed like a
gentleman, he behaves, however, like an antagonistic brute: he threatens Robin

with the stocks. One of Hawthorne's favorite themes, then--the distinction between appearance and reality--receives an early airing, through clothes, in this story. The innkeeper provides another example. He wears a "white apron" (11, 213) and is frequently referred to as "courteous" (11, 214). But his courtesy is like Robin's shrewdness--ironic--and Hawthorne slips us a clothing clue by making the innkeeper's white apron "stained" (11, 213).

The character most likely to be stained--the prostitute--actually receives a sympathetic description. She wears the obligatory sensual "scarlet petticoat" (11, 214) and proffers an attractive figure:

> She was a dainty little figure, with a white neck, round
> arms, and a slender waist, at the extremity of which her
> scarlet petticoat jutted out over a hoop, as if she were
> standing in a balloon. Moreover, her face was oval and
> pretty, her hair dark beneath the little cap, and her
> bright eyes possessed a sly freedom, which triumphed over
> those of Robin (11, 217).

Again, contrast operates. The arm of the law which "saves" Robin has a "broad, dull face" (11, 218). Fortunately, Robin later meets the "Gentleman in his prime, of open, intelligent, cheerful, and altogether prepossessing countenance" (11, 224). All this attention to features by Hawthorne prepares readers for the final, lengthy physical description, that of Major Molineux.

This description of Major Molineux evokes almost the same cathartic reaction from readers as from Robin himself, whose "knees shook, and his hair bristled, with a mixture of pity and terror" (11, 229). For the Major clearly represents fallen grandeur and shaken humanity:

> He was an elderly man, of large and majestic person, and
> strong, square features, betokening a steady soul; but

steady as it was, his enemies had found the means to shake
it. His face was pale as death, and far more ghastly; the
broad forehead was contracted in his agony, so that his
eyebrows formed one grizzled line; his eyes were red and
wild, and the foam hung white upon his quivering lip. His
whole frame was agitated by a quick, and continual tremor,
which his pride strove to quell, even in those
circumstances of overwhelming humiliation. . . . [His]
head . . . had grown grey in honor (11, 229).

He is a man alone. As Paul points out, Major Molineux lives in a state of
"childlessness, and apparent wifelessness";[38] he lives in a foreign and
hostile nation; he lives almost forgotten by his own nation. The nephew he
has offered to help now laughs at him, rejects him. No wonder his strong
physical features quiver. Such physical features allow Hawthorne to sketch
his characters economically and accurately. In this story, Hawthorne, then,
makes considerable use of physical appearance, artifacts, and vocal tones.
And, as has already been noted several times, he periodically describes body
clues--the body revealing emotion. In particular, he focuses on facial clues.
Sometimes these clues threaten and penetrate Robin as when "the leader turned
himself in the saddle, and fixed his glance full upon the country youth . . .
Robin . . . freed his eyes from those fiery ones . . ." (11, 228). Sometimes
these clues reveal the superior knowledge of other characters, as when the
kind gentleman twice accompanies his remarks with a knowing smile (11, 224 and
11, 230). As Sheldon W. Liebman illustrates, Hawthorne specifically looks
into eyes and has those eyes look out at readers because he "is concerned with
insight, vision, and consciousness. . . ."[39] In one sense, Robin sees a great
deal--but seeing is not always knowing. Indeed, even strong young country
eyes can have problems of perception when faced with new sights and deceiving
lights.

Hawthorne also makes some use of the other nonverbal signs and codes--regulators, adaptors, touch, space, and time--although in a much more limited manner. He seems to regulate exchanges in the dialogues by the large number of questions and exclamations from Robin and others. Both these forms of address leave little doubt as to when a character has finished speaking. Robin's stroking of his oaken cudgel might qualify as an adaptor (the manipulation of a prop)--especially as he only uses it once for a practical purpose (barring the muffled stranger's passage). Robin initially touches and is later touched--by a hand and by reality. In his first encounter, Robin reveals his insecurity through touch: "Robin laid hold of the skirt of the old man's coat . . ." (11, 210); as he questions him, Robin retains "his hold of the skirt" (11, 210); only when the man has finished his wrathful rebuke does Robin release "the old man's skirt" (11, 211). The message of touch clearly contradicts the bold tones. Another weakness in Robin is revealed by touch, too: "So saying the fair and hospitable dame took our hero by the hand; and though the touch was light, and the force was gentleness . . . yet the slender waisted woman, in the scarlet petticoat, proved stronger than the athletic country youth" (11, 218). Her touch is one of relative kindness--as is the touch of the only other person to befriend Robin. The old man prevents Robin from leaving the route of his kinsman by "laying his hand on the skirt of . . . [Robin's] grey coat" (11, 226). Later, Robin returns to reality with the help of a question and a touch: "'Well, Robin, are you dreaming?' inquired the gentleman, laying his hand on the youth's shoulder" (11, 230). Because of his experiences, Robin lets go; he no longer needs to cling to coattails.

His dreamlike state has been accentuated by Hawthorne's slight but skillful use of space and time. "We note," says Newman, "that the story does not deal in public space and time but rearranges its materials by means of montage as a dream might."[40] Primarily, space equates with the arrangement of the streets and houses discussed earlier: space, or lack of it, affects and reflects Robin's psyche. Although Robin says that he grows "weary" (11, 231) of town space, his yearning for the wide open country spaces is not altogether convincing. He needs to get oriented to space, to walk the streets with purpose and direction rather than run randomly. He needs, also, to reorient himself to time. At first, things happen quickly. He arrives on the ferry "near nine o'clock" (11, 209). By the time "the ringing bell announced the hour of nine" (11, 215), he has already encountered the man with "hem-hem" on the street and the innkeeper in the tavern! After this, though, he seems to lose his sense of time, for when he meets the kind gentleman, he tells him rather vaguely, "Only an hour or two since, I was told to wait here" (11, 225). Has he dreamed away this time? Hawthorne provides no answer. The onset of daylight, though, promises Robin a chance to gain his bearings, to reset his clock, and to leave the world of dreams.

A reading of the story with attention to the nonverbal details adds a great deal to our understanding of the story. It confirms, for example, the view of the critics who claim that Robin experiences growth and provides concrete evidence to reject those who claim that Robin remains unchanged by the experience. Also, such a reading clarifies many of Robin's emotions and motives. Hawthorne's ambiguity makes this use of a further decoding system--nonverbal signs and codes--a particularly valuable one. Although in his best stories Hawthorne deliberately leaves some mystery, he never fails to drop clues along the way. The kaleidoscope of nonverbal images which flash in Robin's eyes and the sounds which echo in his ears clearly add to his overall confusion--the confusion of a young man for the first time in a town torn by political turmoil. And the nonverbal signs which Robin unknowingly emits can be used by readers to monitor his progress--as long as those readers are on the right wavelength.

A detailed examination of any of his best stories would reveal a similar sensitivity to the place of nonverbal details in his fiction. And even a brief visit, for example, into the streets and forests of Salem to meet Young Goodman Brown provides an example of a variation in Hawthorne's pattern of nonverbal signs and codes. This, too, is an extremely noisy story. Indeed, Edward Wagenknecht hears the sounds of this story as having "been orchestrated . . . almost as elaborately as a tone poem by Richard Strauss."[41] Fogle picks up on a similar note as he listens to "the symphony of sounds" rising "to a wild crescendo."[42] Although this noise of Goodman Brown's forest may be louder than the noise in Robin Molineux's city streets, its tones are not quite as helpful. Certainly, subtle sounds and tempered tones exist. Faith, for example, first speaks in a two-shaded tone which exposes, through its sensuality, what she possesses and, through its sadness, what she will inevitably lose--a young, naive husband: "Whispered she, softly and rather sadly, when her lips were close to his ear" (10, 74). In Hall's spacial scheme, she alone is allowed into the personal territory where whispering works. Even after the forest experience, she continues to be allowed into this space--often enough, at least, to produce "children and grandchildren, a goodly procession" (10, 90). But this offers little comfort for readers who remember Goodman Brown's diverse, nonverbal vocabulary; for example, "Often, awakening suddenly at midnight, he shrank from the bosom of Faith, and at morning or eventide, when the family knelt down at prayer, he scowled, and muttered to himself, and gazed sternly at his wife, and turned away" (10, 89). Hawthorne controls the ending, in part by directing the emotive force not through words but through Brown's other language. As Edward J. Gallagher concludes, "Hawthorne treats Brown's death neither as the time of triumph for the godly, nor as the time of the solace of annihilation for the tortured; and his sonorous but studiedly objective language here simply does not encourage emotional commitment."[43] Beneath that objective language, however, another revealing language operates.

Overall, the tones used by characters in this story, although emotional, are neither emotionally charged nor significantly differentiated. No real progression of tones exists as it does in "My Kinsman, Major Molineux." "Replied" and "cried" occur repeatedly and are used to describe the tones of several different characters. However, such a pattern draws attention when Hawthorne departs from it or adds to it. For instance, he denotes the significance of Goodman Brown's first encounter in the woods through addition and explanation: "replied the young man, with a tremor in his voice, caused by the sudden appearance of his companion, though not wholly unexpected" (10, 76). And Hawthorne prepares readers for a climactic and noisy scene by using the same key tonal word for Goodman Brown as he does for Robin: "shouted Goodman Brown in a voice of agony and desperation; and the echoes of the forest mocked him . . ." (10, 82). This mocking sound of the forest precipitates laughter "loud and long" (10, 83) in Goodman Brown; like Robin, he tries to laugh the "loudest" (10, 83). The source of his laughter is "despair" (10, 83). The message from his laughter, says Dusenbery, is that "The degree of corruption may be measured by the violence of the explosive laughter."[44] The echoes from his laughter again come from the demonic forest:

> The whole forest was peopled with frightful sounds; the
> creaking of the trees, the howling of wild beasts, and the
> yell of Indians; while, sometimes, the wind tolled like a
> distant church-bell, and sometimes gave a broad roar
> around the traveller, as if all Nature were laughing him
> to scorn (10, 83).

Such sounds, whether real or imagined, contribute to this confusion and, in part, reveal his ambivalence--the ambivalence of the lure and fear of evil.

Nowhere are these countermanding cadences so loud and so confused as when the devil's congregation sings a hymn:

> Another verse of the hymn arose, a slow and mournful strain, such as the pious love, but joined to words which expressed all that our nature can conceive of sin, and darkly hinted at far more. Unfathomable to mere mortals is the love of fiends. Verse after verse was sung, and still the chorus of the desert swelled between like the deepest tone of a mighty organ. And, with the final peal of that dreadful anthem, there came a sound, as if the roaring wind, the rushing streams, the howling beasts, and every other voice of the unconverted wilderness, were mingling and according with the voice of guilty man, in homage to the prince of all (10, 86).

In this passage, Hawthorne provides a sense of the noise, but no words. He interprets for readers in his ambiguous way: "hymn . . . love . . . sin . . . fiends . . . verse . . . chorus . . . organ . . . peal . . . dreadful anthem . . . roaring wind . . . rushing streams . . . howling beasts." It is Hawthorne, in fact, who does most of the dark hinting. Echoes rebound throughout the story; in the final paragraph, for example, readers learn that "On the Sabbath-day, when the congregation were singing a holy psalm, he could not listen, because an anthem of sin rushed loudly upon his ear, and drowned all the blessed strain" (10, 89). As Fogle suggests, "This ambiguity permits the author to make free of the two opposed worlds of actuality and imagination without incongruity or the need to commit himself entirely to either."[45]

To add to Goodman Brown's--and readers'--sense of uncertainty, Hawthorne again makes skillful use of artifacts. As in "My Kinsman, Major Molineux," lighting plays a major role in the story. Hawthorne shades his story with natural lights and floods it with artificial lights. The environment of the forest aids in this: Goodman Brown "had taken a dreary road, darkened by all the gloomiest trees of the forest" (10, 75). And the forest gets lit at the altar "by the blaze of hell-kindled torches" (10, 87). These are no spotlights, however; Goodman Brown cannot see--and Hawthorne doesn't help him much, for his narrator cannot see everything either. The narrator admits that what he sees of Goodman Brown's companion is "as nearly as could be discerned" (10, 76); he confesses, none too authoritatively, that the moving staff "must have been an ocular deception assisted by the uncertain light" (10, 76). he observes that "either the sudden gleams of light, flashing over the obscure field, bedazzled Goodman Brown, or he recognized a score of the church-members of Salem Village" (10, 85). The natural and artificial light come together when "four blazing pines threw up a loftier flame, and obscurely discovered shapes and visages of horror on the smoke wreaths . . ." (10, 86). But even this light doesn't help the narrator who asks tantalizing questions rather than providing conclusive answers: "A basin was hollowed, naturally, in the rock. Did it contain water, reddened by the lurid light? or was it blood? or, perchance, a liquid flame" (10, 88). Such tentativeness leads Fogle to proclaim that "This device of multiple choice, or ambiguity, is the very essence of Hawthorne's tale."[46]

The noises, environment, and lighting all add up to the ambiguity and change once Goodman Brown calls out to Faith to resist:

> When Faith obeyed, he knew not. Hardly had he spoken, when
> he found himself amid calm night and solitude, listening
> to a roar of the wind, which died heavily away through the
> forest. He staggered against the rock and felt it chill

and damp, while a hanging twig, that had been all on fire, besprinkled his cheek with the coldest dew (10, 88).

This paragraph serves as a transition between the dark, hellish forest and the light, sunny village.[47] But the transition doesn't help Goodman Brown. As David B. Kesterson says of this paragraph:

> The darkness of the forest, the coldness of the rock and the dew signify the cold, gloomy life which Brown will lead henceforth. The raucous noises, the turbulences of the woods, and the uncanny fire which leaves its fuel cold and clammy symbolize the abnormality of his decision to spend the rest of his life obsessed with sin. Brown's mind becomes dark and poisonous, as unhealthy as the bewitched forest itself.[48]

Certainly the bewitching noises and the beguiling sights have had an impact on Goodman Brown. Like Robin, his senses have been pushed beyond saturation. Unlike Robin, he cannot cope with all that he has heard and seen.

The devastating impact can partially be measured through observing his body clues--which are more pronounced in Goodman Brown than in the less-disturbed Robin Molineux. The former cannot control his face. For instance, as he walks along the road, "he glanced fearfully behind him" (10, 75); he looks at his companion "with a stare of amazement" (10, 77); he reveals his surprise at finding Goody Cloyse in the woods when he "cast up his eyes in astonishment" (10, 79). In the final paragraphs, he wears his distress on his face. He comes into town "staring around him like a bewildered man" (10, 88). He meets Faith "gazing anxiously forth" (10, 89) and "looked sternly and sadly into her face" (10, 89). He "gazed sternly" (10, 89) at Faith when he looked at her at night. Such gazing can, according to Michael Argyle and Mark Cook, "indicate hostility--the essential element appears to be the deliberate breaking of the social norm."[49] Goodman Brown undoubtedly contravenes many social norms after his return from the forest.

Goodman Brown also reveals his emotions through his lack of muscle control. As he thinks of Faith in the woods, "he trembled" (10, 85). As he comes forward in the woods, he finds himself "trembling before that unhallowed altar" (10, 87). As he stands there with Faith, he gazes, receives a gaze, and trembles: "The husband cast one look at his pale wife, and Faith at him. What polluted wretches would the next glance show them to each other, shuddering alike at what they disclosed and what they saw!" (10, 88). Even his trembling, though, suggests ambiguity. He may tremble simply--and most understandably-- from fear. But, on the other hand, he may tremble--if Crews is correct in his analysis of the story--from sexual excitement. Or perhaps, in his ambivalence, he may tremble for both reasons. As Crews puts it, "Brown remains the little boy who has heard rumors about the polluted pleasures of adults, and who wants to learn more about them despite or because . . . he finds them disgusting. His forest journey . . . amounts to a vicarious and lurid sexual adventure."[50] Whatever the reason for it, there's no doubting the depth of his disturbance. Unlike Robin, he never recovers.

For one thing, he receives no solace from friendly touch. He does, unconvincingly, suggest that after his one night in the forest, he will return to Faith and "cling to her skirts" (10, 75). He never does. Hawthorne also makes little use of space or time--although, of course, the events do start at sunset and the companion does magically manage to get from Boston to Salem in under fifteen minutes. Nor does he give much indication of regulators in the dialogue--although he shows his awareness of their existence when the elder person makes a comment to Goodman Brown after "interpreting his pause" (10, 77). Nor does he sprinkle his story with many adaptors--although the black staff and maple branch take on some adaptive elements. All of this is parallel with his use of nonverbal codes and signs in "My Kinsman, Major Molineux": he consistently favors some over others.

One major difference, however, is the relative dearth of physical description in "Young Goodman Brown." We only know that Faith has a "pretty head" (10, 74); that Goodman Brown is young and resembles in expression and clothes his companion--whom our helpful narrator fails to describe; that Goody Cloyse is "a female figure" (10, 78) who cackles; that Martha Carrier is "a rampant hag" (10, 86); that the crowd in the forest is "a grave and dark-clad company" (10, 84). As with the vocal tones, Hawthorne avoids particulars in this story. The unreality and vagueness increase the nightmarish atmosphere of the story. "Had Goodman Brown fallen asleep in the forest, and only dreamed a wild dream of witchmeeting?" (10, 89). It seems likely. But an adornment presents problems: Faith's pink ribbons. Mentioned five times in all, the appearance of the ribbons in the woods would seem to be concrete evidence that something occurred. Fogle thinks not: "If Goodman Brown is dreaming the ribbon may be taken as part and parcel of his dream. . . . This pink ribbon appears in his wife's hair once more as she meets him on his return to Salem the next morning."[51] Ribbon or no ribbon, dream or no dream, the effect remains the same: "instantaneous and devastating," "clear but frightening"--"the loss of religious faith and faith in all other human beings."[52] As the nonverbal elements confirm, Robin stands to awake in daylight while Goodman Brown stands to suffer to death in "gloom" (10, 90).

The nonverbal in Hawthorne, then, is pronounced and follows a somewhat consistent pattern. He undoubtedly possessed an exceedingly keen ear with a perceptiveness for what tones could unveil. His obsession for the ambiguities of laughter should not prevent readers from listening to the edge in his characters' voices. True, there are stories like "Ethan Brand" where laughter dominates and, along with the furnaces, sets the disturbing tone. But in stories like "My Kinsman, Major Molineux," the less dramatic tones prove the most revealing--even to the extent of assessing Robin's growth. Hawthorne is worth listening to.

Hawthorne is also worth watching. For although his eyes may not be as sharp as his ears are keen, he does make considerable use of body clues. He seems to comprehend the inherent possibilities in characters' minor movements for revealing emotion. His blatant allegory has, to some extent, distracted critics from his more subtle techniques. Naturally, much attention has been given to the body clues of a story like "The Minister's Black Veil" where the very meaning depends on an understanding of the consequences of hiding one's face. But even in their discussions of this story, the critics have too often been seduced into trying to unveil the reason for the Minister's actions rather than concentrating on the consequences of them. After all, Hawthorne has shown in stories like "Young Goodman Brown" and "Roger Malvin's Burial" that whether a character has sinned or not matters little; what matters is that once that character believes he has sinned, the human psyche overpowers him with guilt and all its horrible consequences--consequences which affect others, too. The minister, for instance, disturbs his congregation in part because he has violated the social norm of involvement through open facial contact by wearing a simple veil.

Although Hawthorne doesn't clothe many characters in veils, he does, good Puritan heritage being what it was, clothe them. His selection of garments and his attention to features and other aspects of physical appearance are also worth watching. In a novel like The Scarlet Letter, Hester's embroidery cannot possibly go unnoticed. But too often the physical appearance of characters in the short stories receives scant attention. Yet it may be more important in the shorter fiction where economy is of the essence. Rappaccini, for example, in "Rappaccini's Daughter," can be captured in two sentences:

> His figure soon emerged into view, and showed itself to be that of no common laborer, but a tall, emaciated, sallow, and sickly-looking man, dressed in a scholar's garb of black. He was beyond the middle term of life, with grey hair, a thin grey beard, and a face singularly marked with intellect and cultivation, but which could never, even in his more youthful days, have expressed much warmth of heart. (10, 95).

That's Rappaccini.

The other nonverbal code that Hawthorne builds on is artifacts. Interestingly, most of his stories occur outdoors and so the settings are either a natural environment (for example, woods) or the exteriors of buildings and streets. These can, and often do, take on symbolic meaning (the edenic garden in "Rappaccini's Daughter," the devilish hollow in "The Hollow of the Three Hills"), just as physical features frequently do. These settings, as we have seen, gain much from the various lighting schemes Hawthorne employs. Whether it be moonlight, sunlight, or torchlight, the light more often obfuscates than clarifies--allowing Hawthorne to play the type of light tricks with appearance and reality that were to become the trademark of the stage and films in a later age.

Such tricks also explain Hawthorne's use of time and space. He usually gives his stories a specific historical context but then time within the story itself frequently becomes less distinct, less real. The same is true of space. If readers were to trace, say, the footsteps of Robin through the town or the running heels of Goodman Brown through the forest, they would not find many straight paths. These and other Hawthorne characters are disoriented, and time and space provide two of the best means for revealing such disorientation. Overall, regulators and adaptors, then, are the only nonverbal classifications or codes little used by Hawthorne.

What, then, does attention to the nonverbal elements add to the reading of Hawthorne's short fiction? Above all else, such an approach focuses attention on the details of the stories themselves. Surface realities can only lead to inner truths if those realities themselves can first be comprehended. And many of these realities are indeed nonverbal ones. Hawthorne loves to tantalize: Dreams. Light. Dark. Shadows. Hawthorne loves a tentative vocabulary: "Perhaps." "Either . . . or." "Maybe." Yet he also leaves clues which need to be followed. As with the ending of "My Kinsman, Major Molineux," these clues can provide evidence for arriving at an informed judgment. In essence, this is what Fogle calls the masterful "combination of clarity of technique . . . with ambiguity of meaning."[53] And ambiguity may be just what attracted Hawthorne to human nonverbal behavior. All the research in the field confirms the difficulty of deciphering the nonverbal. The nonverbal deals in probabilities. That's ambiguous. In addition to thematic attractions, the nonverbal provides Hawthorne with the artistic necessities of brevity and unity within his shorter fiction. The capturing of the essence of a character through just one repeated nonverbal trait, for example, provides Hawthorne with one method for brevity. The consistent pattern of nonverbal details, such as the importance of all vocal tones, provides him with one means for unity. This overall technique, whether consciously used or not, adds to the structural integrity of his mastering an infant genre. As Fogle, full of praise, phrases it: "His amalgamation of . . . . elements reveals consummate artistic economy in fitting the means to the attempted ends."[54] Replace the ellipsis with the word "nonverbal", and imagine Hawthorne pondering the phrase. After thinking about it, he would have expressed, in an appropriate tone of voice, of course, his agreement.

Perhaps.

Notes

[1] Mary Rohrberger, "Hawthorne's Literary Theory and the Nature of His Short Stories," *Studies in Short Fiction*, 3 (1965), 25.

[2] Nathaniel Hawthorne, "The Haunted Mind," in *Twice-Told Tales*, The Centenary Edition of the Works of Nathaniel Hawthorne, Vol. 9, eds. William Charvat, Roy Harvey Pearce, and Claude M. Simpson (Columbus: Ohio State Univ. Press, 1974), 305. All further references from Hawthorne's works will be included in the text and will cite both the volume and page numbers of the relevant Centenary edition text; volume 10 is *Mosses from an Old Manse* and volume 11 is *The Snow Image and Uncollected Tales*.

[3] Rohrberger, p. 28.

[4] Rohrberger, p. 23.

[5] Simon O. Lesser, "The Image of the Father: A Reading of 'My Kinsman, Major Molineux' and 'I Want to Know Why,'" *Partisan Review*, 22, (1955), 381.

[6] Louis Paul, "A Psychoanalytic Reading of Hawthorne's 'Major Molineux'" The Father Manque and the Protege Manque," *American Imago*, 18 (1961), 279.

[7] Roy Harvey Pearce, "Robin Molineux on the Analyst's Couch: A Note on the Limits of Psychoanalytic Criticism," *Criticism*, 1 (1959), 90.

[8] Edwin Haviland Miller, "'My Kinsman, Major Molineux': The Playful Art of Nathaniel Hawthorne," *ESQ*, 24 (1978), 145.

[9] Frederick C. Crews, *The Sins of the Fathers: Hawthorne's Psychological Themes* (New York: Oxford Univ. Press, 1966), p. 78. See also: Roger P. Wallins, "Robin and the Narrator in 'My Kinsman, Major Molineux,'" *Studies in Short Fiction*, 12 (1975), 173-79.

[10] Miller, p. 146. See also Sheldon W. Liebman, "Robin's Conversion: The Design of 'My Kinsman, Major Molineux,'" *Studies in Short Fiction*, 8 (1971), 457.

[11] Paul, p. 280.

[12] Richard Harter Fogle, *Hawthorne's Fiction: The Light and Dark* (Norman: Univ. of Oklahoma Press, 1964), p. 104.

[13] Robert Dusenbery, "Hawthorne's Merry Company: The Anatomy of Laughter in the Tales and Short Stories," *PMLA*, 82 (1967), 285.

[14] Franklin B. Newman, "'My Kinsman, Major Molineux': An Interpretation," *The Univ. of Kansas City Review*, 21 (1955), 209.

[15] Fogle, p. 111.

[16] Daniel E. Hoffman, *Form and Fable in American Fiction* (New York: Oxford Univ. Press, 1961), p. 119. See also pp. 113-25 and Liebman, p. 450 and note 8 on p. 450.

[17] Dusenbery, p. 285.

[18] Mary Allen, "Smiles and Laughter in Hawthorne," *Philological Quarterly*. 52 (1973), 121.

[19] Allen, p. 128.

[20] Allen, p. 119.

[21] J.A.R.A.M. Van Hooff, "A Comparative Approach to the Phylogeny of Laughter and Smiling," in *Non-verbal Communication*, ed. R.A. Hinde (Cambridge: Cambridge Univ. Press, 1972), p. 209.

[22] See Van Hooff's review of theories on the primitive origins of laughter, p. 211. See also pp. 209 and 210.

[23] Miller, p. 145.

[24] Wallins, pp. 174-75.

[25] Two were imprisoned, one was supposedly "driven from the province by the whizzing of a musket ball" (11, 208), and one reportedly died a premature death from the pressures of his job.

[26] Miller, p. 68.

[27] R.J. Andrew commenting on Van Hooff's article, p. 239.

[28] Van Hooff, p. 209.

[29] Thomas E. Connors, "'My Kinsman, Major Molineux': A Reading," *Modern Language Notes*, 74 (1959), 301.

[30] Dennis Brown, "Literature and Existential Psychoanalysis: 'My Kinsman, Major Molineux' and 'Young Goodman Brown,'" *The Canadian Review of American Studies*, 4 (1973), 68-69.

[31] For other links to Shakespeare's play (Robin's name, for example), see Connors, note 2, p. 299.

[32] Wallins, p. 179. See Wallins, pp. 173-79, for the best discussion of the use of shrewdness; the analysis above is based, in part, on Wallin's observations.

[33] "Resolute" and "resolve" seem to replace "shrewd" and "shrewdness" as the catchwords at this point. See in particular, pp. 219-20.

[34] See, for example, Michael Argyle and Mark Cook, *Gaze and Mutual Gaze* (Cambridge: Cambridge Univ. Press, 1975), pp. 74-75 and 92-93.

[35] J.C. Nitzsche, "House Symbolism in Hawthorne's 'My Kinsman, Major Molineux,'" *The American Transcendental Quarterly*, 38 (1978), 172-73.

[36] Nitzsche, p. 167.

[37] The ferryman, at the beginning of the story, for example, "lifted a lantern, by the aid of which, and the newly risen moon, he took a very accurate survey of the stranger's figure" (11, 209); the watchman, in the middle of the story, "carried a lantern, needlessly aiding his sister luminary in the heavens" (11, 218); the participants in the parade, at the end of the story, "disturbed the moonbeams . . . [with] a dense multitude of torches . . . concealing by their glare whatever object they illuminated" (11, 227).

[38] Paul, p. 284.

[39] Liebman, p. 451.

[40] Newman, p. 205.

[41] Edward Wagenknecht, *Nathaniel Hawthorne: Man and Writer* (New York: Oxford Univ. Press, 1961), pp. 40-41.

[42] Fogle, p. 29.

[43] Edward J. Gallagher, "The Concluding Paragraph of 'Young Goodman Brown,'" *Studies in Short Fiction*, 12 (1975), 30.

[44] Dusenbery, p. 286.

[45] Fogle, p. 21.

[46] Fogle, p. 16.

[47] See Reginald Cook, "The Forest of Goodman Brown's Night: A Reading of Hawthorne's 'Young Goodman Brown,'" *The New England Quarterly*, 43 (1970), 473-81 for a full discussion of the contrasting elements of the environment.

[48] David B. Kesterson, "Nature and Theme in 'Young Goodman Brown,'" *The Dickinson Review*, 2 (1970), 43.

[49] Argyle and Cook, p. 75.

[50] Crews, p. 102. It is worth noting that "high dames," "wives," "widows," and "ancient maidens" don't tremble in the forest but "fair young girls...trembled, lest their mothers should espy them" (10, 85).

[51] Fogle, p. 18.

[52] See, respectively, Fogle, p. 18; Cook, p. 473; and D.M. McKeithan, "Hawthorne's 'Young Goodman Brown': An Interpretation," *Modern Language Notes*, 67 (1952), 93.

[53] Fogle, p. 32.

[54] Fogle, p. 22.

Chapter 4
SILENT ERNEST

"I...was searching for the unnoticed things that made emotions."

> Ernest Hemingway in *The Paris Review*
> interview.

By the time of Ernest Hemingway, the short story was no longer an infant genre. And yet the elements of brevity and unity remained important, although somewhat formulaically applied. Hemingway, though, shattered the pat formulas and took brevity and unity to previously uncharted depths, often using nonverbal moments as his depth-finder. Like Hawthorne, Hemingway presented ambiguity in his work and his life--although his ambiguities had a more deceptive quality about them. Deceptive, in part, because of the apparent simplicity of the author, his style, and his heroes. Aspects of Hemingway invited this. Undoubtedly, he struck a pose and created an image of athletic prowess, sexual vigor, drunken violence, and rugged experience. There was another side to Hemingway, though. As Philip Young puts it, "Fist and rose, both were real."[1]

His style supposedly supports the public image, the image supposedly supports the style, and both have fascinated critics from the reverent all the way to the hostile. The Hemingway style has become a literary obsession. It has been lauded as the best in American fiction, damned as the worst in male chauvinism, and parodied as the most recognizable target in English. The characteristics of that style--his economy, his mastery of dialogue--have been analyzed by linguists and tabulated by word counters. At its best, style

should enhance or reveal meaning, and Hemingway's does. His style is his way
of meaning. He writes simple sentences, but he does not write simply. Few
critics, though, have explored an essential ingredient of that deceptively
simple style: Hemingway's superb use of the nonverbal--a stylistic device at
least as economical, at least as evocative, and at least as eloquent as his
verbal language.

As with Hawthorne, vocal tones serve as a revealing starting point.
Unlike Hawthorne, Hemingway, to the surprise of some, proves to be a much
quieter writer--even a silent writer on occasion. H. E. Bates, for instance,
summarizes the radical and important break Hemingway makes from the convention
of commenting on tones:

> In this convention the words of a character had their
> intonation, flavor, emotion, or measuring underlined by
> the writer . . . Hemingway swept every letter of that
> convention away. In its place he put nothing but his own
> ability to imply by the choice, association, and order of
> the words, whether a character was feeling and speaking
> with anger, regret, desperation, tenderness; quickly or
> slowly ironically or bitterly. . . . Hemingway asked
> nothing except the cooperation of the reader in the job of
> capturing these intonations and emotions.[2]

What readers have to do, however, is respond to all the nonverbal clues,
sparse though they may seem. Then readers may indeed begin to "feel something
more than they understood"[3] in Hemingway.

These clues exist outside the dialogues themselves. But even Hemingway's
preciseness with verbal elements has been questioned. Michael F. Moloney, for
instance, points out "the bare bleakness of the conversation"; he then
comments that "One may legitimately question the accuracy of his ear for the

nuances of speech."[4] Arthur Waldhorn concurs; he suggests that Hemingway's use of dialogue fails when it is isolated, "which is perhaps why he fares so badly on the screen, where he has been represented almost exclusively by his dialogue--and it sounds absurdly artificial."[5] And yet Hemingway's dialogue clearly works within the context of his written story. Indeed, both Moloney and Waldhorn go on to acknowledge this point. The former concedes that "the fact remains that the kind of effect he wants he superbly achieves."[6] The latter confesses that "on the page, where his dialogue has a unique visual authenticity that makes the words look as if the sound, the speech pattern is but one among many facets of Hemingway's expression that fuse to sustain tension and stretch meaning."[7] Both critics, though, struggle when they seek to comprehend and explain this success. Eudora Welty doesn't even try. To her, "Hemingway's use of conversation . . . is an obscuring and at the same time a magical touch; it illuminates from the side. It makes us aware of the fact that communication is going on."[8] Part of Hemingway's magic is his ability to conjure up the nonverbal elements. Silently.

Silence--perhaps the ultimate nonverbal signal--often speaks loudly in Hemingway's fiction. This vast, ambiguous lexicon of silence rarely means nothing. As anthropologist William J. Samarin acutely analogizes: "Silence can have meaning. Like the zero in mathematics, it is an absence with a function."[9] That function, along with many other aspects of Hemingway's nonverbal dexterity, can be seen in two quite different Hemingway short stories: "The Killers" and "Hills Like White Elephants." Ironically, these two short stories are best known for their dialogue. But in both stories, dialogue punctuates silence, not the other way round. Silence and the length of silence combine to reveal. Hemingway employs a clock in one story and a timetable in the other to tick-tock away the psychologically damaging minutes more than to record the hour. However, if we take a stopwatch to his clocks, we see a significant lapse between telling time and clock time.

Time tortures Nick in--and beyond--"The Killers." In this tale, Hemingway conveniently hangs a clock on the wall of the lunch-room. This clock, however, runs a little fast ("It's twenty minutes fast"),[10] just as Nick does at the end of the story: "I'm going to get out of this town" (289). And perhaps the clock runs fast because it is behind the times; after all, Henry's lunch-room once served as "a saloon" (282). The clock continues to show "bar time"--set fast to have more time to move customers at closing time. It is not the only discordant, possibly anachronistic element: Henry's lunch-room is operated by a George and Mrs. Hirsch's boarding house by a Mrs. Bell. There are some disturbing minor disorientations which foreshadow the major events that seriously disorient and distress the young and impressionable Nick Adams.[11]

Yet "the events" of the story are really divisible into three non-events: Ole does not arrive at Henry's, Nick does not persuade Ole at Hirsch's, and the reaction back at Henry's is not unified. Once again, silences and other nonverbal elements enhance and reveal the meaning of these non-events. Let's look at that clock again.[12] Why? Well, because it's wrong. And because "George [repeatedly] looked at the clock" (284). Hemingway draws our attention to time by repetition and discrepancy, by the constant need to solve the mathematical riddle. If the little hand points to the five and the big hand points to the eight and the clock is twenty minutes fast, what time is it? Hemingway further complicates the clock by the repeated use of his favorite pronoun, "it." Does "it" in "It was a quarter past six (284)" refer to the actual time or to the clock time? Careful readers have to pause to contemplate this wrinkle in the riddle.

The gangsters arrive, like a "vaudeville team," at about five ("'The clock says twenty minutes past five'" [279]); they leave at about six fifty ("The clock marked . . . five minutes past seven. 'Better give him five minutes'" [285]). Their attempts at tough gangster dialogue would have consumed only a tiny portion of the one hour and fifty minutes. For much of this time, Nick stays bound to the cook "back to back in the corner, a towel tied in each of their mouths" (284): neither can talk. Al sits nearby with "a sawed-off shotgun" (284). Nick thinks. Silently. And how slowly silent time passes, causing, as the nonverbal research suggests, greater and greater anxiety: the "swagger" (286) at his release only affirms the fear he has felt. But nothing has really happened. Ole chooses not to dine out that evening; he, too, has been waiting. Silently.

Hemingway's narrator doesn't give us much help with the silences--or anything else. Once again, he doesn't tell us when they occur or how long they last. But they exist and we must make of them what we can. As Bates said of Hemingway, he is "a man with an ax,"[13] and here the ax has fallen on the narrator to the extent that Carl Ficken calls him "practically effaced."[14] Nowhere is the narrator more effaced than in presenting the dialogue. The most toneless of all vocal verbs--"said"--suffices nearly a hundred times. Once the narrator does give us a clue to the tone of the said: "'Say,' he said. 'What the hell?' He was trying to swagger it off" (286). Even this doesn't say much. Once, and only once, does he provide us with a tonal description: Ole "talked in the same flat voice" (288). Once, instead of reporting the complete dialogue, the narrator presents its gist: "George explained that the cook was sick"(285). Occasionally, the monotony breaks with an "explained" (279), a "called" (282), a "went on" (287), and even some specific silences--"Ole Andreson said nothing" (287); "Ole did not say anything" (287); "They did not say anything" (289).

Nearly as often as the narrator uses "he said," he withholds description between interchanges of dialogue. This would suggest that Hemingway understood regulators. For example, Mrs. Bell ends one of her sentences with a rhetorical twist: "'He was in the ring, you know.' 'I know it'" (288). But his most frequent regulator of dialogue is the question. In this short story of ten and a half pages, seventy-two questions are asked by various characters; on only fourteen of these occasions does the narrator use "asked." Questions clearly mark the progress and process of dialogue. They also raise a question. Were seventy-two pieces of information really needed by the characters? No. The barrage of questions and constant chatter help to reveal the levels of anxiety--especially in the gangsters.

Too often only stereotypical aspects of Al and Max generate comment. In one of the deservedly most famous interpretations of the story, Cleanth Brooks and Robert Penn Warren mention the "unreal and theatrical quality"; they go on to discuss "the dialogue" of the gangsters with its "sleazy quality of mechanized gag and wisecrack" as revealing "their professional casualness" and "contempt and boredom."[15] Two other critics, in two deservedly lesser known interpretations, echo this analysis. Leo Gurko suggests that "the two killers . . . embody destructiveness in its purest form."[16] Jackson J. Benson points out that the "two Chicago hoodlums . . . have set up Henry's lunchroom for the kill in anticipation of Ole's nightly visit" with "unemotional efficiency."[17] First, a couple of factual quibbles. The killer's destructiveness, although not the point of the story, is never proved. Indeed, considerable ambiguity surrounds the contract. Why, for instance, didn't they go straight to Ole's to make the "hit"? The lunch-room stakeout, far from being efficient, seems unduly complicated and exposes them to a number of witnesses--and fails because Ole doesn't show up. (George suggests that Ole doesn't come nightly.)

Furthermore, what delays them when they leave the lunch-room? Nick not only walks to Ole's, but he also spends time there: yet no killers arrive.

Beyond the factual, though, questions about the emotional stability of the killers remain because of the number and type of questions they ask, because of their physical appearance, and because of their body clues. One has to wonder, for example, if they really came to do a job in a town without knowing its name.[18] And despite the lengthy silences, one also has to wonder about their compulsion for spurts of chatter. In fact, Max is the real talker. Al tells him: "You talk too goddam much" (283); "It's sloppy. You talk too much" (285); and "You talk too much, all the same" (285). As Richard W. Lid illustrates, "In Hemingway to speak is to lose something."[19] Max at first responds that he has to keep George "amused" but later poses a question: "We got to keep amused, haven't we?" (285). This and other questions signal his uncertainty. In place of his positive term "amused," we could justifiably use the negative "to keep from getting anxious." For they are anxious.

Their physical appearance suggests just how anxious they are--and, even more importantly, how their anxiety amplifies Nick's. Initially nameless and faceless, the gangsters eventually receive the fullest description of any characters. In fact, Nick and George remain undescribed; Sam is a "nigger" with an "apron" (282); Mrs. Bell is "the woman" (286, 287, 288) or "the landlady" (288); and Ole is a "big man" (287) with a prizefighter's "face" (288). That's all. Al and Max, however, have clothes, features, and builds for us and Nick to notice. Al "wore a derby hat and a black overcoat buttoned across the chest. His face was small and white and he had tight lips. He wore a silk muffler and gloves" (280). This gangster tries to look the part by wearing a black coat, an ostentatious muffler (an ominous word for a gangster on a contract), and tight gloves. His face would cause anxiety, too, with its unwelcoming color and uninviting lips. Max doesn't look any more reassuring. "He was about the same size as Al. Their faces were different, but they were dressed like twins. Both wore overcoats too tight for them" (280). Hemingway progressively adds information--just as Nick would probably progressively notice things about them. Here Hemingway reveals that their fitting clothes don't fit--suggesting that the gangster roles and task they have chosen may not fit either. A little later, he reveals that "the same size" means small ("the other little man" [280]). These mean little men seek to kill a "big man": Ole "had been a heavyweight prizefighter and he was too long for the bed" (287). Al's "sawed-off shotgun" (284) which makes "a slight bulge under the waist of his too tight-fitting overcoat" (285) also makes them both brave--and wounds Nick.

Although "In their tight overcoats and derby hats" the gangsters may have "looked like a vaudeville team" (285), no one laughs. Nor should anyone, because this team, far from being professional and predictable as most critics claim, are all the more disturbing because they work so hard at being real gangsters.

Their body clues are disturbing, too. Max, we suspect, continually looks in the mirror (282, 282, 282, 285) not just for the practical purpose of seeing Ole come in--he could, after all, have sat facing the door--but also to ease his own insecurity, his own self-imposed image of the complete gangster. "The man called Max sat at the counter opposite George. He didn't look at George but looked in the mirror . . ." (281). His avoiding George's eyes foreshadows Ole's later refusal to meet Nick's eyes and may suggest Max's lack of confidence. His nerves are clearly on edge. When George watches him eat, Max reacts:

> "What are *you* looking at?" Max looked at George.
> "Nothing."
> "The hell you were. You were looking at me."

"Maybe the boy meant it for a joke, Max," Al said.

George laughed.

"*You* don't have to laugh," Max said to him. "You
don't have to laugh at all, see?" (281).

George has done well not to laugh earlier when he watched both gangsters
eating "with their gloves on" (281). Brooks and Warren helpfully point out
that they eat with their gloves on "to avoid leaving fingerprints."[20] But
would professional "hit men" worry about fingerprints and not three
eye-witnesses? Or would professional "hit men" even take a chance on having to
eliminate eye-witnesses? No. These "hit men" are neither comic nor mechanical.
According to the nonverbal clues, these "hit men" are the most frightening
kind: the nervous, often irrational, inexperienced gangsters trying to be
macho mobsters. That's one reason Hemingway devotes so much of his script to
them. Another reason? Hemingway has an adolescent audience for this horror
show: Nick.

Before the night is over, Nick hurries to a second showing. The theatre
moves from lunch-room to boarding house. Bathed in arc-light and braced with
courage, Nick goes to warn Ole of the apparently impending "hit." The
narrator describes the environment with great numerical accuracy: "Three
houses up the street was Hirsch's rooming-house. Nick walked up two steps and
pushed the bell" (286). In going to Ole, Nick acts with responsibility, but
he fails to comprehend the ex-prizefighter's refusal to leave his corner, his
apparent throwing in of the towel. Ole, it seems, will neither fight nor run.
Hemingway gives two nonverbal clues to Ole's inertia--his posture and his
gaze:

> Ole Andreson was lying on the bed . . . with his head on
> two pillows. He did not look at Nick. . . . He looked at
> the wall. . . . Ole Andreson rolled over toward the wall
> . . . He said, talking to the wall. . . . He looked at the
> wall. . . . He did look toward Nick. . . . Nick went out.
> As he shut the door he saw Ole Andreson with all his
> clothes on, lying on the bed looking at the wall (287-88).

The very rhythm of the passage suggests the pounding of a head against a blank brick wall--which exactly parallels Nick's experience.

Ole's refusal to open his posture to Nick reveals his immersion in an unchanging emotion. That emotion may not just be mere resignation to the inevitable, either. Ole's actions--or once again, more accurately, his absence of action--may fit what psychiatrist Joost Meerloo has characterized as "a passive . . . defense mechanism . . . the passive surrender to danger. The person possessed by . . . fear and anxiety, instead of fleeing from or fighting the danger, surrendered, blended, and collaborated with the dreaded instance."[21] Part of Ole wants to run; part of Ole wants to surrender. The conflicting desires paralyze him. Ole thinks. Silently. And how slowly silent time passes.

The troubled Ole not only rests almost immobile on the bed, but he also avoids Nick's eyes. Without the essential eye-contact, Ole and Nick cannot communicate. Ole intends this: he faces an inner wall as well. Troubled by the threat of loss and riddled with anxiety, he needs to escape Nick's gaze to avoid real involvement with him. As Dr. Morris D. Reimer diagnoses "the averted gaze," it helps "overcome the underlying suffering and . . . [is] of great unconscious value as a defensive measure."[22] Nick, though, suffers from no apparent threat. Still, Nick suffers. He suffers, among other things, from receiving no sign of involvement from Ole; and although he may not be conscious of it, Nick's psyche will suffer from this and other non-events.

Erving Goffman points out that the receiver of "improper behavior" inevitably suffers more in the long run than the refuser of proper behavior.[23] By preferring the wall's blank gaze to Nick's concerned eyes, Ole sentences them both to anxiety. Nick has been, as Mordecai Marcus puts it, "confronted with . . . despairing passivity in the behavior of the prizefighter Andreson."[24] This has been a dark night: when Nick travels from Henry's to Ole's, he moves from a lighted street into a dark "side street" (286); when he leaves Ole's to return to Henry's, "he walked up the dark street" (288) to the artificially lighted street. The environment mirrors his experience.

His return to the world of the lunch-room (now noticeably referred to, for the first time, as an "eating house" [288]) shows part of his disturbance. Ole rooms and now lives at "the end of a corridor" (286); Nick returns and now suffers in a lunch-room with easy exits. Commenting on this and other Hemingway locales, Earl Rovit observes that Hemingway "frequently . . . explicitly and implicitly used the image of 'the clean well-lighted place' as the arena of conflict, the dramatic locus of an onslaught or a challenge."[25] Nick moves from Ole's curious unwillingness to be involved with life to the cook's literal and figurative "shut[ting] the door" (288) on involvement. Sam, although previously bound to Nick, has always reacted differently. When Nick swaggers after being gagged, Sam simply "felt the corners of his mouth with his thumbs" (286). When Nick wonders about warning Ole, Sam advises against it; when Nick decides to go anyway, "The cook turned away" (286). The cook's territory is the kitchen; Nick's place is at "the other end of the counter" (279); George's space is "back of the counter" (288).

From his position, both real and status, George copes better--although he, too, carefully avoids involvement; he projects a useful phlegmatism. "George's attitude throughout," Gurko comments, "sets the standard. . . . George rejects noninvolvement; at the same time he keeps his balance and composure."[26] Although George may provide a model through his ability to survive, he hardly becomes actively involved. For instance, he doesn't go to warn Ole; he sends Nick: "'Listen,' George said to Nick. 'You better go see Ole Andreson'" (286). And he later silences the conversation with Nick and discourages the final dialogue with contrived industry: "George reached down for a towel and wiped the counter" (289). The gangsters had also used a towel to silence Nick: it silences him better the first time. For Nick reopens the conversation, realizes he wants to leave town, and receives sound but futile advice: "'Well,' said George, 'you better not think about it.'"(289). But, as Young tells us, "Nick, far from being calloused, is an extremely sensitive, even an abnormally sensitive human being."[27] All of Hemingway's wide array of nonverbal clues support Young's reading. Those long minutes of captive fear at the hands of erratic gangsters, those empty words from the mouth of a former prizefighter, and that imagined final fatal moment will not be easily forgotten. "It's too damned awful" (289).

By focusing on the moment itself, Hemingway frequently forces readers to ponder about the past and project into the future. What, for instance, had Ole once done to deserve his current contract? Perhaps he failed to throw a fight. Perhaps. It's ambiguous. It doesn't matter, though, for, as with Hawthorne's dream or no dream technique, the effect remains the same. What will become of Nick? We need to read the rest of the Nick stories to find the answer; Young did and concludes that "The man will die a thousand times before his death, but from his wounds he would never recover. . . ."[28] Other Hemingway characters suffer, too, in the spotlight of a single moment where only shadows fall on the past and into the future. The shadowiest spotlighted story of this type may be "Hills Like White Elephants." Indeed, Frank O'Connor in one of the most interesting and one of the least complimentary commentaries on the story complains that "The light is admirably focused but it is too blinding." Part of O'Connor's difficulty with the story comes because it provides no background information, which, he claims, forces readers into making a moral judgment "on an abstract level."[29] But the clues are there and so, too, in his own way is Hemingway.

Unfortunately, too many critics have taken the apparent objectivity at face value rather than questioning why so many readers end with similar conclusions about the story if, as Bates pronounces, "Hemingway makes no single attempt to influence the readers' thoughts, impressions, or conclusions. He himself is never there; not for a single instant does he come between object and reader."[30] Wrong. Hemingway and his narrator may be effaced, but they are not obliterated. As in "The Killers," the narrator does manage to set time and tone in the story without ever seeming to. The story opens with the narrator crisply and precisely setting the chronological and topographical scene in the opening paragraph. We are told that the train would arrive "in forty minutes" (273) and would halt "for two minutes" (273). Such precision mirrors the prose with apparently crisp dialogue dominating the printed page. Apart from describing the girl's two visions of the countryside, the ordering and receiving of the inevitable drinks, and the moving of the bags, the allegedly objective and almost anonymous narrator introduces the characters through their words, their silences, and their nonverbal language. They reveal themselves by what they say--and fail to say. Physical description of characters, for example, does not exist. The waitress is "the woman" (273); the couple is referred to as "The American and the girl with him" (273). He calls her by name, or nickname, once: "It's really an awfully simple operation, Jig" (275). Significantly, he uses her personal name when broaching the nearly unbroachable for the first time.[31]

Toward the end of the story, the time frame is completed by the serving woman who comes through the barrier of bamboo beads to announce: "The train comes in five minutes" (277). To underline this important fact, Hemingway chooses to have the man repeat it as a translation:

> "What did she say?" asked the girl.
> "That the train is coming in five minutes" (277).

So, thirty-five minutes have passed as the two talked--occasionally. If spoken as a continuous dialogue, their exchange would consume no more than three to four minutes of clock time. Therefore, at least thirty-one unaccounted minutes have passed. How can we account for such a gap in the narration? Perhaps the narrator has chosen only to emphasize the crucial dialogue and has, by choice and necessity, omitted other dialogue and action. But it seems more likely--given the narrator's penchant for precision and detail--that the time has been spent in deafening silence. This silence confirms what the dialogue suggests: they fail to communicate on all but the most superficial level.

Although the narrator rarely informs us directly of the silences, his clear references to clock time and the consistent verbal failures of the couple imply long periods of quiet. Again, we cannot tell precisely when they occur; we cannot tell how long each one lasts. But we do know who makes the best use of the silence: the woman. Hemingway uses artifacts to control our sympathies. Offering three different perspectives on the natural environment, the narrator, the girl, and the American reveal something about themselves. The story opens with the narrator setting the scene:

> The hills across the valley of the Ebro were long and
> white. On this side there was no shade and no trees and

> the station was between two lines of rails in the sun.
> Close against the side of the station there was the warm
> shadow of the building and a curtain, made of a string of
> bamboo beads, hung across the open door into the bar, to
> keep out flies. The American and the girl with him sat at
> a table in the shade, outside the building. It was very
> hot . . . (273).

We get the picture precisely. A few lines later, the narrator tells us, through a masterful display of distancing, that the woman looks at the girl who looks at the hills. Yet before the girl comments on the hills, the narrator takes, accurately, factually, and economically, a zoomshot of just the hills and the countryside: "They were white in the sun and the country was brown and dry" (273). The narrator sees what he sees.

She sees much more: "They look like white elephants" (273). Using her imagination, she conjures up visions of elephants from the shape of hills. Using his mind, the American denies such nonsense: "I've never seen one" (273). He sees nothing. Their incompatibility looms (already at this early stage of the story) larger than any elephant. So does her willingness to submit. "'They're lovely hills,' she said. 'They don't really look like white elephants. I just meant the coloring of their skin through the trees'" (274). And towards the end of the story, the narrator completes the picture by telling us what the girl is looking at on the other side:

> The girl stood up and walked to the far end of the
> station. Across, on the other side, were fields of grain
> and trees along the banks of the Ebro. Far away, beyond
> the river were mountains. The shadow of a cloud moved
> across the field of grain and she saw the river through
> the trees (276).

She sees contrast and space; she faces a choice. In Lionel Trilling's words, "When she looks in one direction, she sees the landscape of sterility; when she looks in the other direction, she sees the landscape of peace and fecundity."[32] Her choice? "They sat down at the table and the girl looked across at the hills on the dry side of the valley . . ." (277). She surrenders; she submits.

She submits, though, only after a dialogue which dramatizes the differences and emphasizes her feeling of entrapment. The undertones of this dialogue reverberate much louder than the words and combine with the silences to define a desperate atmosphere; Bates concludes that the result is a story which "is one of the most terrible Hemingway or anyone else ever wrote."[33] Quoting F. O. Matthiesen on Henry James, Richard Bridgman perceptively detects a parallel in these seemingly disparate authors; Matthiesen comments that James had "the ability so to handle a conversation that he keeps in the air not merely what is said, but what isn't--the passage of thoughts without words."[34] And the extensive communication failure in this story leads to favorite anthology questions: "The main topic of discussion between the man and girl is never named. What is the 'awfully simple operation'? Why is it not named?"[35] Abortion. Because they can't face or talk about things. A+. But there's more. Too much can be made of the impending abortion, just as too much can be made of, say, the caesarean in Hemingway's "Indian Camp": neither event is "the point" of its respective story. This couple avoids meaningful communication about anything. Their lives consist "of new drinks" (274) (which often taste bitter), looking "at things" (274) (which they cannot agree on), and spending nights in hotels (which they cannot recall): "nada."

The control of the dialogue comes again through regulating questions, avoiding descriptive adverbs, and eliminating many verbs. In all, twenty-five questions are asked. Revealingly, the girl asks over two-thirds of them. She

desperately seeks reassurances about their future together without the baby.
He predictably responds with correct but convictionless answers:

> "But I know it's perfectly simple."
> "And you really want to?"
> "I think it's the best thing to do. But I don't want you
> to do it if you don't really want to."
> "And if I do it you'll be happy and things will be like
> they were and you'll love me?"
> "I love you now. You know I love you."
> "I know. But if I do it, then it will be nice again if I
> say things are like white elephants, and you'll like it?"
> "I'll love it. I love it now but I just can't think about
> it. You know how I get when I worry."
> "If I do it you won't ever worry?"
> "I won't worry about that because it's perfectly simple"
> (275).

This is damning dialogue. She asks meaningful questions: he responds with
platitudinous answers. She reveals that once things were better ("it will be
nice again . . ."); he reveals his selfishness ("You know how I get when I
worry"). Hemingway in this exchange provides no adverbs to describe the tones
of voice--indeed, he doesn't even provide the traditional verbs ("said," for
example). In fact, nearly three-quarters of the exchanges in this story occur
without a verb interrupting the flow. When Hemingway does use a verb, it is
as toneless as in "The Killers"--mostly "said," with a few "askeds," and one
"called." But a remarkable fact remains: we can hear clearly both of their
tones. Lionel Trilling explains how and what he hears in the story:

> Hemingway has no need to supply the description of his
> [the man's] tone of voice as he urges the girl to consent
> to the abortion--the rhythm of his sentences, the kinds of

words he uses, makes plain what his tone is. You cannot
say "really" and "just" (in the sense of *merely*) as often
as he does without sounding insincere.

Nor do we need the girl's tones of voice labelled for us.
We understand that she is referring to a desire which she
does not know how to defend in words and that therefore
she speaks in bitterness and irony.[36]

The sharp edge of tones that echo tonelessly cuts as deeply as the silences
that sound deafening until, in Bridgman's words, "Hemingway's dialogue . . .
began contracting and kept on until at last it dwindled down to silence, the
other side of speech."[37]

Several other deft, nonverbal touches polish this story--and lead us to
know that the narrator may not be quite as objective as he would have us
believe. He clearly controls our responses somehow, for we end up despising
the man and sympathizing with the woman. True, her dilemma seems most
serious; her imagination appears more fertile; her voice sounds less
self-serving. But to help us further, the narrator slips us several body
clues and two adverbs in a story of scrupulously pared language. First, the
body clues. The girl does a lot of looking. She tries to look beyond her
present existence--but without real success. Her looking becomes almost a
refrain in the story (273, 273, 274, 275, 275, 277) and serves to show her
discomfiture with the dialogue ("The girl looked at the ground the table legs
rested on" [275]) and her greater vision ("The girl looked across at the hills
. . . and the man looked at her and at the table" [277]). She looks either at
the hills or at the bead curtains; he looks at the bags with the "labels on
them from all the hotels where they had spent nights" (277). She looks at a
possible future; he looks at an impossible past. More incompatibility.

Not only does the girl look longingly, but she also opens the curtains on her emotions. She first observes the writing on the bamboo bead curtains and her natural curiosity makes her ask what it says; when she finds out that it spells the name of a drink, she wants to try an "Anis del Toro" (274). Gary D. Elliott somehow sees a lot more in the curtains: "The bamboo beads are the key to the girl's lack of enthusiasm about her lover's urging an abortion because the bead curtain represents and functions as a rosary for this young woman who must certainly be a Catholic. She resists an abortion because her religious heritage adamantly opposes such action."[38] This tendency to turn Hemingway into a theologian also struck Gurko when writing on "The Killers"; he reports that "symbolists have had a field day . . . , seeing in it a reworking of Christian legend, with Ole Andreson (son of man) the Christ figure pursued and killed by the Devil's agents, while Nick Adams (Adam--the original man) tries vainly to prevent it."[39] Such ingenuity in finding a religious schema in Hemingway does his art a disservice. That bead curtain keeps the flies out, Hemingway's narrator tells us, but not, apparently, the critics. Its other function has to do with a nonverbal moment: "The girl looked at the bead curtain, put her hand out and took hold of two of the strings of beads" (275). This occurs right in the middle of the critical discussion about their potential for future happiness and suggests her uncertainty about the verbal exchange. She uses the beads as an adaptor; they serve no practical purpose for the girl. But her seeking relief from tension in playing with the beads speaks loudly to readers. Change Elliott's rosary beads into worry beads.

She has good reason to worry--as two adverbs, one used by narrator for the man and the other attached to describe a facial display of the girl's, confirm. When the man, having deposited the bags at "the other tracks" (277), having failed in his vision again ("He looked up the tracks but could not see the train" [277]), and having reverted to drinking Anis, observes the people at the bar, he notes that they seem to be waiting "reasonably" (278). When the girl smiles at the woman who has just told him that the train will arrive soon, she smiles "brightly" (277). These words seal our responses to the two characters and our convictions about their incompatibility.

As Trilling has pointed out, the man's observation, through the narrator, of people "waiting reasonably for the train" (278) reveals more about himself than the people: it satisfied his self-serving, self-justifying nature. Those reasonable people reflect, he feels, his strength and her shortcoming. He has been waiting for the train--and the abortion--reasonably, rationally. She has been waiting for the train by describing hills like white elephants and by mentally denying the abortion: how unreasonable. Clearly he is blind to much more than the hills. Clearly Hemingway is capable, contrary to many critical viewpoints, of depicting man's "insensitivity to woman's needs."[40]

And although Jig may not be as blind as he, she can see her way only out of the station--not out of nothingness. When she smiles "brightly" at the woman "to thank her" (277) for the news, we sense that this is a smile of both gratitude and relief. This serving woman, who does not even speak the same language, comes and goes at will through the bead partition. She brings the welcome news that the long periods of silence and short bursts of dialogue will soon end. Discerning readers suspect the train will bring only a change of place; wherever the couple goes, silence and meaninglessness will follow. And somehow "brightly" seems to confirm our impression of Jig throughout the story: she tries to sparkle in a lackluster relationship. By the end of the story, however, she realizes the futility. After smiling "brightly" at the woman, she smiles twice more--both times at the man, neither time brightly. This lack of expression is the expression. When he announces that he will move the bags, "She smiled at him" (277). When he returns from the bar, "She

. . . smiled at him" (278). Given the contexts, her smiles suggest two things: a woman masking her emotions, a woman submitting. Her smiles give him one message, readers, another. His insensitivity probably leads him to believe she smiles from contentment. We suspect she first smiles to mask her discontent. And from this suspicion, we conclude that there can be no hope for either positive verbal or nonverbal communication. People who hide behind false selves can rarely reach out to one another.

This story of failure ends with nothingness. Some starry-eyed readers believe Jig will leave him and live, with a child, of course, happily ever after. Hemingway does nothing to encourage such a consolatory reading. Indeed, her final smile does not suggest rebellion, but submission. As Jig smiles, she says: "'I feel fine. . . .' 'There's nothing wrong with me. I feel fine'" (278). This is a regrettable regression from her earlier and finer line: "Would you please please please please please please please stop talking?" (277). Mary Ritchie Key claims that females "smile more throughout their lifetime, if they 'learned their lesson well'--that females are supposed to be pleasant. . . ."[41] She further points out that the smile as a "submissive gesture" can also be witnessed in captive chimpanzees, surviving prisoners-of-war, and successful servants. There could be elements of all of these in the Jig of the future.

The dominating dialogue, then, doesn't penetrate deeply. But below and around that dialogue, Hemingway has rooted the story in crucial nonverbal clues. Following essentially the same nonverbal patterns as he did in "The Killers," Hemingway uses, to some degree or another, all but one of the nonverbal classifications and codes: touch. That omission seems particularly appropriate in this story--a story devoid of what touch can represent: intimacy. O'Connor would take this a step further and say that Hemingway and his readers lack intimacy. He complains that "Hemingway . . . has so studied the artful approach to the significant moment that we sometimes end up with too much significance and too little information."[42]

Certainly Hemingway, perhaps even more so than Hawthorne, makes great demands on his readers. In Hawthorne's case, the ambiguity comes from an excess of information; that is, Hawthorne provides choices. In Hemingway's case, the ambiguity comes from an absence of information; that is, Hemingway omits. In both cases, sensitivity to the nonverbal on the readers' part can help make the correct choices and fill in the omissions. The little information, then, is the significance. With the onus on the reader, there will be those readers who will not "have the sensibility or . . . the experience to grasp the key"; Atkins continues that these are usually the same readers "who find satisfaction in the patterned stories of O. Henry and de Maupassant."[43] Hemingway delights in fracturing that comfortable and predictable pattern by replacing it with the often uncomfortable and unpredictable sketch of human behavior. Bates acknowledges that "Hemingway . . . is prepared to trust the reader to absorb the proper impression" through providing a "direct pictorial contact between eye and object, between object and reader."[44] Thus there will be those occasions in Hemingway when, as Gullason says, "the short story may end before the reader really warms to it. And the writer--not the reader--is charged with lack of empathy."[45] Hemingway faced that charge and changed nothing. His best works are brief and seemingly fragmentary. His best works are, in the words of that unlikely admirer, D. H. Lawrence, "so short, like striking a match, lighting a brief sensational cigarette, and it's over."[46]

Hemingway knew and delighted in this aspect of his work. Like the paintings he so admired,[47] his fiction had a life beyond. He told George Plimpton in his famous The Paris Review interview:

If a writer stops observing he is finished. But he does not have to observe consciously nor think how it will be useful. Perhaps that would be true at the beginning. But later everything he sees goes into the great reserve of things he knows or has seen. If it is any use to know it, I always try to write on the principle of the iceberg. There is seven eighths of it under water for every part that shows. Anything you know you can eliminate and it only strengthens your iceberg. It is the part that doesn't show.[48]

Richard P. Adams, in a fascinating article on the links between Hemingway and T. S. Eliot entitled "Sunrise Out of the Wasteland" (in which he discusses, among other things, the parallel between Eliot's theory of the "objective correlative" and Hemingway's comments in *Death in the Afternoon*), develops what Hemingway's comments and works signify. "Hemingway's implication . . . [is] that prose, like poetry, can be symbolic; that it may be made to carry overtones of feeling and meaning, partly conscious, partly unconscious, that will give it rich and permanent esthetic value."[49] The only troubling word here is "symbolic." If by this he means that what we do nonverbally has symbolic value, then he is correct--for the author undeniably has his characters send nonverbal messages. When a systematic nonverbal approach is taken by readers of literature, the messages received become conscious ones. But that is not to say that readers don't receive some of these messages unconsciously. If by "symbolic" Adams means what some call the traditional literary symbols (for example, the ketchup in "The Killers" being symbolic of blood), then he has missed the subtlety that is Hemingway's.

As we have seen in both stories used as illustration here--and could see in many other Hemingway stories--Hemingway reaches far beyond the bounds of dialogue to create his artistic effect. And yet he continues to fool critics as perceptive as Brooks and Warren who, commenting on "The Killers," erroneously look at the printed page instead of into the words; they suggest that "practically all information . . . [is] conveyed in simple realistic dialogue."[50] Then they proceed in the rest of the paragraph to document some of the nonverbal moments! A nonverbal approach to Hemingway is particularly profitable because, as Robert Daniel illustrates, "Hemingway's heroes never give complete [verbal] expression to their feelings. . . ." Indeed, what the reader has to accomplish is the adoption of "the required attitude" from noticing "two or three traits"[51] in Hemingway's characters. Most readers acknowledge Hemingway's considerable power. But too often, only his power is acknowledged. He also writes with an unerring sensitivity to the subtleties of human nonverbal behavior and the emotions this behavior reveals. Hemingway uses the unspoken to suggest all the voices and kinds of language operating at every level of the human psyche: this enriches his fiction. And much of this richness comes from those slight movements which are not slight moments in Hemingway. This is an important and much neglected part of his genius--and of his style. For he did not just present speech patterns or represent a way of life. Nor did he guess about unarticulated motivation or suggestive movement. These, too, he knew how to say. Silently.

Notes

[1] Philip Young, "Focus on *To Have and Have Not*, to Have Not: Tough Luck," in *Tough Guy Writers of the Thirties*, Crosscurrents Modern Critiques Series, ed. David Madden (Carbondale: Southern Illinois Univ. Press, 1968), p. 42.

[2] H. E. Bates, "Hemingway's Short Stories" in *The Modern Short Story* (London: Thomas Nelson, 1942); rpt. in *Hemingway and His Critics: An International Anthology*, American Century Series, ed. Carlos Baker (New York: Hill and Wang, 1961), pp. 74-75.

[3] Ernest Hemingway, *A Moveable Feast* (New York: Charles Scribner's Sons, 1964), p. 75.

[4] Michael F. Moloney, "Ernest Hemingway: The Missing Third Dimension" in *Fifty Years of the American Novel*, ed. Harold C. Gardiner (New York: Charles Scribner's Sons, 1951); rpt. in Baker, p. 184. See also Richard W. Lid, "Hemingway and the Need for Speech," *Modern Fiction Studies*, 8 (1962), 405: "But it is not, for all its colloquial character, the language of real people. It is an imagistic language. . . ."

[5] Arthur Waldhorn, *A Reader's Guide to Ernest Hemingway* (New York: Farrar, Straus and Giroux, 1972), p. 39.

[6] Moloney, pp. 184-85.

[7] Waldhorn, p. 39.

[8] Eudora Welty, "The Reading and Writing of Short Stories," *The Atlantic Monthly*, 183 (February 1949), 46-49 and 54-58; rpt. in *Short Story Theories*, ed. Charles E. May (Columbus: Ohio Univ. Press, 1976), p. 166. Eusebio L. Rodriques, "'Hills Like White Elephants': An Analysis," *Literary Criterion*, 5 (1962), 108, provides a different image: "Hemingway uses dialogue as a composer uses melodic themes."

[9] William J. Samarin, "Language of Silence," *Practical Anthropology*, 12 (1965), 115.

[10] Ernest Hemingway, "The Killers," in *The Short Stories of Ernest Hemingway* (New York: Charles Scribner's Sons, 1938), p. 279. All further references to Hemingway's short stories will be taken from this edition and will be included in the text.

[11] Leo Gurko in *Ernest Hemingway and the Pursuit of Heroism* (New York: Thomas Y. Crowell, 1968), p. 190, notes these disorientations, but in his quest for a longer list becomes disoriented to the facts of the story. Somehow, for example, he finds evidence that Mrs. Bell is "a substitute taking the real landlady's place for the day," and that the gangsters "leave in a rage." The major events in the story do not include Ole's death--despite Gurko's including him in a list of Hemingway characters who "lose their lives" (p. 176).

[12] See William V. Davis, "'The Fell of Dark': The Loss of Time in Hemingway's 'The Killers,'" *Studies in Short Fiction*, 15 (1978), 319-20. Davis concludes that "Hemingway parallels Nick's illumination to the clock time of Henry's establishment. Beyond it, in real time, there is only Nick's walk through the darkness back to Henry's place, just as real time exists beyond and behind the illusion of clock time." See also Charles A. Owen, Jr., "Time and the Contagion of Flight in 'The Killers,'" *Forum*, 3 (1960), 45-46. Owen notes the movement away from using time primarily as a suspense builder, and that "Hemingway's 'The Killers' makes the reader aware of time in a number of ways, each of them adding depth or dimension to the story" (p. 45). See also Robert Daniel, "Hemingway and His Heroes," *Queen's Quarterly*, 54 (1947), 472: "To surround melodramatic action with . . . clocks that don't keep time is to deflate it. . . ." For a complex but careful analysis of time in Hemingway see Frederic I. Carpenter, "Hemingway Achieves the Fifth Dimension" in *American Literature and the Dream* (New York: The Philosophical Library, 1955); rpt. in *Ernest Hemingway: Five Decades of Criticism*, ed. Linda Welshimer Wagner (East Lansing: Michigan State Univ. Press, 1947), pp. 279-87.

[13] Bates, p. 72.

[14] Carl Ficken, "Point of View in the Nick Adams Stories," in *Fitzgerald/Hemingway Annual*, ed. Matthew J. Bruccoli and C. E. Frazer Clark, Jr. (Washington, D.C.: N.C.R., 1971), pp. 212-35; rpt. in *The Short Stories of Ernest Hemingway: Critical Essays*, ed. Jackson J. Benson (Durham, N.C.: Duke Univ. Press, 1975), p. 97.

[15] Cleanth Brooks and Robert Penn Warren, *Understanding Fiction*, 2nd ed. (New York: Appleton-Century-Crofts, 1959), p. 306.

[16] Gurko, p. 189.

[17] Jackson J. Benson, *Hemingway: The Writer's Art of Self-Defense* (Minneapolis: Univ. of Minnesota Press, 1969), p. 142.

[18] Edward Stone, "Some Questions About Hemingway's 'The Killers,'" *Studies in Short Fiction*, 5 (1967), 12-17, raises a whole series of unanswered questions about the story--many of them rather stretched--in his attempt to claim Hemingway transposed a Chicago scene into Summit for thematic reasons. See also Kenneth G. Johnston, "'The Killers': The Background and the Manuscripts," *Studies in Short Fiction*, 19 (Summer 1982), 247-51.

[19] Lid, p. 401.

[20] Brooks and Warren, p. 304. Only Daniel detects the irony inherent in these gangsters: "The very title is a piece of self-mockery" (p. 474).

[21] Joost Meerloo, *Unobtrusive Communication: Essays in Psycholinguistics* (Assen, Netherlands: Van Gorcum, 1964), p. 29.

[22] Morris D. Reimer, "The Averted Gaze," *Psychiatric Quarterly*, 23 (1949), 108.

[23] See Erving Goffman, *Interaction Ritual* (New York: Doubleday, 1967), p. 117.

[24] Mordecai Marcus, "What Is an Initiation Story?" *The Journal of Aesthetics and Art Criticism*, 14 (1960), 221-27; rpt. with revisions in *Short Story Theories*, p. 193.

[25] Earl Rovit, *Ernest Hemingway*, Twayne's United States Authors Series, ed. Sylvia E. Bowman (New York: Twayne Publishers, 1963), p. 116.

[26] Gurko, p. 191.

[27] Philip Young, *Ernest Hemingway, A Reconsideration* (University Park: The Pennsylvania State Univ. Press, 1966), p. 49.

[28] Young, p. 55.

[29] Frank O'Connor, "The Lonely Voice," in *The Lonely Voice: A Study of the Short Story* (Cleveland: The World Publishing Co., 1963); rpt. in *Short Story Theories*, p. 90. See, also, Rodriques, p. 108; he asks: "Is this a story?" and cautions that the story "has to be read as carefully as one reads a poem or a lyric" (p. 109).

[30] Bates, p. 75.

[31] For an analysis of Hemingway's use of personal names in dialogue see Olga K. Garnica, "Rules of Verbal Interaction and Literary Analysis," *Poetics*, 6 (1977), 155-68. Garnica uses Hemingway's "Indian Camp" as an illustration of pragmatics--a variation of regulators.

[32] Lionel Trilling in his "Commentary" on "Hills Like White Elephants," in *The Experience of Literature* (New York: Holt, Rinehart, and Winston, 1967), p. 732. See also Reid Maynard, "Leitmotif and Irony in Hemingway's 'Hills Like White Elephants,'" *University Review*, 37 (1971), 273-75; he calls the story a "prose painting."

[33] Bates, p. 75.

[34] As quoted in Richard Bridgman, "Ernest Hemingway" in *The Colloquial Style in America* (New York: Oxford Univ. Press, 1966), pp. 195-230; rpt. in *Ernest Hemingway: Five Decades of Criticism*, p. 184.

[35] Laurence Perrine, *Literature: Structure, Sound, and Sense* (New York: Harcourt, Brace, 1970), p. 225. See, also, Rodriques, p. 107: "What are they talking about?"

[36] Trilling, p. 731.

[37] Bridgman, p. 186.

[38] Gary D. Elliott, "Hemingway's 'Hills Like White Elephants,'" *The Explicator*, 35 (1977), 22-23. See also Kenneth G. Johnston, "'Hills Like White Elephants': Lean, Vintage Hemingway," *Studies in American Fiction*, 10 (Autumn 1982), 233-38. Among other things, Johnston points out that the story takes place in Spain--a predominantly Catholic country.

[39] Gurko, p. 188.

[40] Alan Holder, "The Other Hemingway," in *Twentieth Century Literature*, 37 (1963), 153-57; rpt. in *Five Decades of Criticism*, p. 105. Holder points out some other stories in which Hemingway displays "a capacity to question some of his own deepest responses towards women" (106-07): *To Have and Have Not*, "Cat in the Rain," and "An Alpine Idyll."

[41] Mary Ritchie Key, *Paralanguage and Kinesics* (Metuchen, N.J.: The Scarecrow Press, 1975), p. 153.

[42] O'Connor, p. 90.

[43] Atkins, pp. 64-65.

[44] Bates, pp. 73-74.

[45] Gullason in *Short Story Theories*, p. 23.

[46] D. H. Lawrence, "In Our Time: A Review," in *Phoenix* (New York: Viking Press, 1936); rpt. in *Hemingway: A Collection of Critical Essays*, The Twentieth Century Views Series (Englewood Cliffs, N.J.: Prentice-Hall, 1962), ed. Robert P. Weeks, p. 93.

[47] See, for example, his comments in Lillian Ross, "How Do You Like It Now Gentlemen?" from *The New Yorker*, 13 (May 1950); rpt. in *Hemingway: A Collection of Critical Essays*, pp. 17-39. Also see a remarkable article by Meyly Chin Hagemann, "Hemingway's Secret: Visual to Verbal Art," *Journal of Modern Literature*, 7 (1979), 87-112.

[48] George Plimpton, "An Interview with Ernest Hemingway," *The Paris Review*, 18 (1958), 60-89; rpt. in *Ernest Hemingway: Five Decades of Criticism,*, p. 35.

[49] Richard P. Adams, "Sunrise Out of the Waste Land," *Tulane Studies in English*, 9 (1959), 119-31; rpt. in *Ernest Hemingway: Five Decades of Criticism*, p. 242.

[50] Brooks and Warren, p. 304.

[51] Daniel, pp. 477 and 485, respectively.

Chapter 5
VISUAL FLANNERY

*"To the hard of hearing you shout, and for the almost
blind you draw large and startling figures."*

Flannery O'Connor, in "The Fiction Writer
and His Country."

Flannery O'Connor creates unforgettably bizarre and memorably grotesque
moments in her fiction. She writes with greater loudness and blatancy than
Hemingway; she confesses her affinity to Hawthorne and to his sense of romance
that reaches beyond one perception of reality.[1] In addition, she proclaims
that she is a writer with Christian concerns who presents the moment of grace
in her fiction.[2] Her uses of the grotesque, of Catholicism, and of the South
have dominated O'Connor criticism.[3] And yet there is much more to her work.
Considerable attention has been paid to her freaks (her "Dickensian devotion
to oddity"[4]), very little to her recognizable family units. A lot of
attention has been paid to her total effect (which is frequently devastating),
very little to the stylistic means of accomplishing that effect. Yet, one of
the main reasons her fiction succeeds is that she uses realistic details as an
index to psychological truth; the revelations in her stories--revelations
frequently unfolded, unleashed, unhinged in a story's climax--test and
illustrate one of her own tenets of fiction-writing: "The greater the story's
strain on the credulity, the more convincing the properties in it have to
be."[5] Many of those properties pertain to the nonverbal.

O'Connor probed the possibilities of this principle in and out of
fiction. Two of her essays in *Mystery and Manners*--"The Nature and Aim of

Fiction" and "Writing Short Stories"--address the importance of concrete detail and focus on the importance of the senses, both to the reader and writer. The senses, she says, demand the concrete because "you cannot appeal to the senses with abstractions." And the nature of those concrete details depends on the "perceptive apparatus" of readers. That apparatus includes perceptiveness of the nonverbal. In O'Connor, two major dimensions exist: "The Sense of Mystery" and "The Sense of Manners." Since the manners make the mystery, the manners take on an importance too rarely realized by those writing about O'Connor's fiction. A significant portion of those "manners" are nonverbal manners and matters, for, as O'Connor put it, "You can't say anything meaningful about the mystery of a personality unless you put that personality in a believable and significant social context."[6] That social context clearly includes regulators, body clues, adaptors, physical appearance, vocal tones, touch, space, time, and artifacts.

Artifacts, in particular, assume a special significance in O'Connor's fiction. Like Hawthorne and Hemingway, she uses all the nonverbal techniques, yet distinctly prefers certain of them. She obviously was intrigued by artifacts, for her work is "a veritable community of objects."[7] Hazel Motes, for instance, in *Wise Blood* wears a blue suit, a black hat, silver-rimmed spectacles, and drives a rat-colored car. These objects, Melvin J. Friedman suggests, have to do with hierophany--the sacred manifested in the ordinary.[8] Certainly, there may be elements of the sacred in her objects, but they accumulate more than religious meaning. In part, O'Connor sees that the real challenge of the short story as opposed to the novel is a necessity of making "the details . . . carry more immediate weight."[9] A study of the artifacts and the other nonverbal techniques in one of O'Connor's own favorite and much anthologized stories, "Good Country People," demonstrates the importance of an awareness of detail--for that detail becomes critical in recognizing what

Kathleen Feeley sees as a vital part of O'Connor's creative imagination: "The idea of falseness in a character."[10] Particularly in this strange story, Friedman feels that the reader has been prepared and warned "of impending ironical twists and turns by an elaborate series of clues."[11] Taking a systematic, nonverbal approach to this story insures that the subtle clues, and not just the blatant ones, catch the reader's eye.

Many of the objects in O'Connor stand up and kick us. Hulga's wooden leg, for instance, makes an "awful noise"[12] throughout most of the story so that readers cannot help but hear it. The victim of a childhood hunting accident, Hulga makes the worst of her wooden leg. O'Connor's diction characterizes a bitter young woman whose movements exaggerate her physical disability: she "stumped into the kitchen" (275), "lumbered into the bathroom" (271), and "slammed the door" (271)--and each one annoys her overly protective mother. Hulga builds an impenetrable barrier against her mother's interference with the sound of ugliness. Named "Joy" by her mother, she changes her name to "Hulga" in what she perceives as "her highest creative act" (275). The name makes Mrs. Hopewell think "of the broad blank hull of a battleship" (274). With a battleship name and a peg leg, Hulga spends her days reading and brooding. Her philosophy of nothingness and her boorish behavior stem from the loss of a physical limb that sets her out on a psychic limb. Thus her physical handicap and appearance take on major significance.

The wooden leg initially accounts for much of her behavior. As Josephine Hendin puts it, "Hulga's maimed body has formed her mind, shaped her identity and turned her life into a reaction against her own body."[13] This is not unusual in O'Connor. Mr. Shiftlet in "The Life You Save May Be Your Own" has one arm; Rufus Johnson in "The Lame Shall Enter First" has a clubfoot; Flannery O'Connor had lupus, the side effects of which put her on crutches. But in her fiction, such handicaps go beyond the physical and the psychological. An object like Hulga's leg takes on symbolic meaning; "the literal," David Eggenschwiler tells us, "is being manipulated for allegorical ends."[14] What does the wooden leg stand for? O'Connor in her essay "Writing Short Stories" suggests that "we perceive that there is a wooden part of [Hulga's] soul that corresponds to her wooden leg."[15] Does this mean, then, that the loss of her wooden leg results in the loss of the wooden part of her soul? Like so many Hawthorne stories, the ending of this O'Connor story is ambiguous, and thus we have to trust the nonverbal approach. Dorothy Walters hopes "that Hulga, having mastered the fundamentals of the fact of evil, is now prepared for additional instruction in spiritual reality";[16] Dorothy Tuck McFarland thinks that the "destruction of her illusions and her defenses . . . may be . . . the means of her salvation";[17] and Eggenschwiler believes that "her old self has been burned away, and she might be forced into a free choice that may be a new beginning. Perhaps it might even lead her to accepting the ironies inherent in man's spiritual-corporeal nature."[18] As in Hawthorne and Hemingway, close attention to nonverbal details helps the reader eliminate much of tentativeness evident in the diction ("may be," "might") of critics who discuss the ending.

Hulga loses her leg in one of O'Connor's most bizarre scenes. Anticipating a seduction by an apparently naive Bible salesman in a hayloft, Hulga actually finds herself in an episode of perversion and revelation when he instead removes, and disappears with, her leg. This loft scene presents a rape. An expected "screw" becomes an unexpected unscrew as "Hulga's venture into sexual initiation leads her to a spiritual rape."[19] Her triumph turns to trauma when Pointer asks for her leg rather than her body. "As sensitive about the artificial leg as a peacock about his tail" (288), Hulga protests--but weakening intellectually, she physically submits seconds later. And yet she manages to hold on to a rational explanation for this reversal:

"She decided that for the first time in her life she was face to face with real innocence. This boy, with an instinct that came from beyond wisdom, had touched the truth about her" (289). Three decidedly non-innocent objects soon dispel this misperception, though. Manley Pointer opens his valise to reveal "a pale blue spotted lining" and "two Bibles" (289). The standard Bible salesman travel kit, however, reveals more than Hulga expected. One of the Bibles is hollowed rather than hallowed and contains "a pocket flask of whiskey, a pack of cards, and a small blue box" (289) that turns out to be a package of contraceptives. These objects, blatant and bizarre as they are, finally force Hulga to reexamine the Bible salesman--and, of greater importance, to look inside herself.

But Hulga has trouble seeing. She has lost her glasses. We find out that Hulga's vision needs glasses early in the story ("the big spectacled Joy-Hulga" [275]; "squint-eyed" [276].) We learn that Pointer likes "girls that wear glasses" (284)--probably because they can't see through him. We watch as he maneuvers: "When her glasses got in his way, he took them off her and slipped them into his pocket" (287). And we realize that she spends her life blind to her surroundings; as she looks out at a hazy landscape, "she didn't realize he had taken her glasses" (287). As Walters points out, Hulga belongs to a long line of O'Connor characters who remain "oblivious to the beauties about them."[20] To Hulga without glasses, the sky looks "hollow," the ridge looks "black," and two fields look like "green swelling lakes" (287). To Hulga without glasses and without a wooden leg, the disappearing Pointer looks like a "blue figure struggling successfully over the green speckled lake" (291). Such a detail sends the Christian allusionist critics into ecstasy. Here is "Christ walking on the water."[21] Maybe. But the fact remains that Hulga's vision is still blurred. This may well be better than the clearer but scornful vision that her glasses had given her. Will the purchase of a new pair of glasses promise any more meaningful vision?[22] Her "churning face" (291) at least suggests that her complacency has been shattered.

O'Connor often relies on faces (and other physical appearances) as keys to the attitudes and emotions behind them. As Hendin puts it, she writes "about people trapped within their own bodies, figuratively drowning in their own juices."[23] Her character, Mr. Shiftlet, in "The Life You Save May Be Your Own," expresses the body's limitation: "The body, lady, is like a house; it don't go anywhere: but the spirit, lady, is like an automobile: always on the move, always . . ." (152).[24] Almost without exception, O'Connor's concept of the body troubles the critics--perhaps no critic more so than Martha Stephens:

> For what is oppressive about the O'Connor work as a whole, what is sometimes intolerable, is her stubborn refusal to see any good, any beauty or dignity or meaning, in ordinary human life on earth. A good indication of what must be called O'Connor's contempt for ordinary human life is the loathing with which she apparently contemplated the human body. . . . Human beings are ugly in every way; the human form itself is distinctly unpleasant to behold; human life is a sordid, almost unrelievedly hideous affair. The only human act that is worthy of respect is the act of renouncing all worldly involvement, pleasure, and achievement.[25]

Bodies in O'Connor do lack beauty. But Stephens is overreacting and misreading. O'Connor uses the body primarily to show its limitations and to reveal how all too often it shapes personality and limits the spirit. Nowhere does she simply advocate renouncing the body and this world. She seeks to force us, however, to take a look beyond our bodies and outside of this world.

Hulga at the outset does neither. First described as "a large blonde girl who had an artificial leg" (271), Hulga seems to will her body and her self into further ugliness. She has "the look of someone who has achieved blindness by an act of will and means to keep it" (273). When asked by her mother to go for a walk, Hulga's "remarks were usually so ugly and her face so glum" (274) that Mrs. Hopewell would relent. Her mother feels that Hulga becomes more and more "bloated, rude, and squint-eyed" (276) and refused to acknowledge that "if she would only keep herself up a little, she wouldn't be so bad looking. There was nothing wrong with her face that a pleasant expression wouldn't help" (275). Much of Hulga's appearance, however, comes as a direct response to her mother.

The more her mother treats her "still as a child," the more childish she becomes. O'Connor carefully dresses her characters in clothing that Walters believes "serves as a summary of personality, a comic reflection of an unchanging inner sense of self."[26] Hulga "went about all day in a six-year-old skirt and a yellow sweat shirt with a faded cowboy on a horse embossed on it" (276). The skirt belongs to an earlier age; the sweat shirt represents a faded past that she can no longer (since losing her leg at age ten "in a hunting accident" [274]) enjoy. Both items of clothing annoy her mother: "Mrs. Hopewell thought it was idiotic and showed simply that she was still a child" (275). When the "child" seeks to prove her intellectual womanhood, she changes clothes to go on her date. But her inexperience and incapacity show. She puts on "a pair of slacks and a dirty white shirt, and as an afterthought, she had put some Vapex on the collar of it since she did not own any perfume" (284). She comes home with one pant-leg empty and with the shirt much more stained: she both loses and gains from the experience.

The experience comes to her doorstep in the guise of a Bible salesman. Manley Pointer (another self-chosen name) also has a revealing physical appearance. "He was a tall gaunt hatless youth. . . . He was not a bad-looking young man though he had on a bright blue suit and yellow socks that were not pulled up far enough. He had prominent face bones and a streak of sticky-looking brown hair falling across his forehead" (277). His ectomorphic build suggests a suspiciousness, detachedness, and introspectiveness not altogether evident from his early dialogue; his clothing colors mirror the frequent sky and sun in O'Connor; in this story, "the sky was . . . cold blue" (287) and the sun shines into the loft.[27] Pointer eventually brings some clarity and light into Hulga's non-life. And although initially his wisdom is almost hidden ("yellow socks sucked down in his shoes from walking" [285]), he eventually unveils a wisdom far beyond a Ph.D. in Philosophy: "You ain't so smart. I been believing in nothing ever since I was born!" (291). His superior wisdom about people has been clear to readers throughout from his nonverbal clues and O'Connor's suggestions about his deceptiveness. But Hulga closes her eyes and her mind to his behavior. When he wears a "new and wide-brimmed" hat, that "was toast-colored with a red and white band around it and was slightly too large for him" (285), she assumes that it is for her benefit--and ultimately it is, but not in the way she anticipates.

Both Mrs. Hopewell and Hulga seem blind to Pointer's depravity. Their reactions to him and assumptions about him highlight their inability to see beyond the superficial, to see through the mask of country simplicity that he slips on as astutely as he later slips off Hulga's leg. Though physical and intellectual opposites, both mother and daughter regard Pointer from superior stances. Hulga imagines playing intellectual games with him; Mrs. Hopewell becomes comfortable with him from the moment he utters the magic words, "country people" (278); she feels superior to country people--although her record with tenants suggests they feel even more comfortable with her. They both fail to detect his body clues and vocal tones; the alert readers notices them and anticipates the reversal of Hulga's hopes.

Manley Pointer has mastered the manipulation of his face. O'Connor makes sure that we at least spot his deceptiveness: "pretending to look puzzled but with his eyes sparkling" (277); "under cover of a pant, he fell forward into her hall" (277). With the astuteness of a salesman--especially one who has to sell Bibles--he can change his demeanor instantly: "he laughed . . . and then all at once his face sobered completely. He paused and gave her a straight earnest look . . ." (278). By contrast, Mrs. Hopewell gives herself away with her posture--"stiffening slightly" (278)--when she lies about her Bible. As he starts to talk about God, she tries to regulate the conversation with a classic indication that she is ending the dialogue: "She stood up" (278). He rejects the regulation: "He didn't get up" (278). He has learned persistence, to feel out his clients all the while letting his words and body speak with apparent sincerity: "He began to twist his hands and looking down at them, he said softly, 'Well lady, I'll tell you the truth . . .'" (278). And, as her dinner waits, he feeds her insatiable appetite for superiority, pausing occasionally to see if he strikes a responsive chord ("He glanced up into her unfriendly face" [278]). He does strike the right note with his country simplicity and receives a medley of Mrs. Hopewell's finest platitudes in return: "'Why!' she cried, 'good country people are the salt of the earth! Besides, we all have different ways of doing, it takes all kinds to make the world go round. That's life!'" (279). Her vocal tones--"cried," "stirred" (279)--reveal her animation, both to us and to Pointer: "His face had brightened" (279). Having detected that he now has more than his foot in the door, he continues to press his advantage by using his verbal and nonverbal dexterity and by reading her verbal and nonverbal responses.

He underscores his assumed affinity by dramatically "lowering his voice" (279) and telling her that he has a terminal heart condition and regulating this news by trailing off his sentence: "He paused, with his mouth open, and stared at her" (279). As so often in O'Connor, eyes talk. His words and stare result in "her eyes . . . filling with tears" (279). Distracted by his eyes and her tears, she "murmured" (279) an uncharacteristically generous and immediately regretted invitation to dinner. Master actor that he is, Pointer modulates his voice to an "abashed" (279) tone. His talents have not only got him invited to dinner, but by associating himself with good country people (the Freemans) and identifying himself with the physically afflicted (Hulga and her weak heart), they have also created an opening for his later perverted deviltry.

The target of his perversion, Hulga, has to be won over during dinner. His simplicity seduces her intellectually. After an initial "look" (280), Hulga pretends to ignore him; she "had not glanced at him again" (280)--not directly, perhaps, but later in the passage we learn that she has been "observing sidewise" (280) his behavior; he, in turn, "would dart a keen appraising glance at the girl as if he were trying to attract her attention" (280). O'Connor, as she often does, controls whether the dialogue is direct or indirect. In this instance, she uses indirect dialogue by summarizing the substance of his life history in her own abbreviated version rather than recording every word of his actual lengthy dialogue: "'He who losest his life shall find it,' he said simply and he was so sincere, so genuine and earnest that Mrs. Hopewell would not for the world have smiled" (280). His deception has been masterful; through perception of weakness, he manipulates verbally and nonverbally.

Yet despite deception and perception, he cannot hide all his body clues nor disguise all his vocal tones. Nor does O'Connor intend for him to deceive her readers--only the characters in the story. Fortunately for Pointer, the physical appearance of his face--"bony and sweaty and bright, with a little pointed nose in the center of it" (283)--draws our attention, and Hulga's to his telling gaze:

> His look was different from what it had been at the dinner table. He was gazing at her with open curiosity, with fascination, like a child watching a new fantastic animal at the zoo, and he was breathing as if he had run a great distance to reach her. His gaze seemed somehow familiar but she could not think where she had been regarded with it before (283).

But careful readers recall Mrs. Freeman's fascination with Hulga's artificial leg and her "special fondness for the details of secret infections, hidden deformities, assaults upon children" (275). O'Connor again lets eyes tell as well as see: Mrs. Freeman has "beady steel-pointed eyes" (275); Manley Pointer has eyes "like two steel spikes" (289). To draw out attention to the importance of eyes, O'Connor begins the story looking into Mrs. Freeman's "black eyes" (271) and metaphorically motorized expressions: she has a "neutral expression" (271) when alone, and "forward and reverse" (271) gears for dealing with people. And the story ends with Mrs. Hopewell's eyes "squinting" (291), as Mrs. Freeman's "gaze drove forward" (291).

What do these eyes and gazes reveal? They tell us, in part, of an affinity between Mrs. Freeman and Manley Pointer--an affinity with its roots in perversion. Unconsciously perceptive, Mrs. Hopewell classifies both Pointer and Mrs. Freeman as "good country people" (270 and 272 respectively), but fails to realize that their continuous blending does not lie in goodness. Consciously superior, Mrs. Freeman can see absolutely no similarity between herself and Pointer. O'Connor affirms Mrs. Freeman's unseeing nature with the last words of the story. Mrs. Freeman refers to Pointer: "Some can't be that simple. . . . I know I never could" (291). Fooled by his simplicity and unaware of his duplicity, Mrs. Freeman defines herself in misdefining Manley Pointer.

She is not alone, however, in misunderstanding Pointer. Hulga and her mother also miss the point of his eyes. This is not all that the Hopewells share. Although they appear to be intellectual worlds apart, they both squint. And, in a moment of crisis, Hulga, "almost pleading" (290), drops into the dialect of her mother: "Aren't you just good country people?" (290). Pointer's uncontrolled gaze should have warned Hulga. In a review of research on gazing, Argyle and Cook indicate that abnormal gazes function "as a threat signal"; such staring "constitutes a bizarre piece of rule-breaking, whose meaning is unclear, from which the person stared at might well want to escape."[28] Unless she feels protected by a Ph.D. in philosophy.

Hulga uses her academic background to consider his unacademic question: "You ever ate a chicken that was two days old?" (283). And she initially retains an icy control over her voice and her expressions: "The girl's expression remained exactly the same" (283); "in a flat voice she said . . ." (283); "The girl stood blank and solid and silent" (283). In contrast, O'Connor helps Pointer modulate his voice ("he said triumphantly" [283]; "he asked softly" [283]; "he murmured" [284]) and vary his expressions: he "shook all over with little nervous giggles, getting very red in the face, and subsiding finally into his gaze of complete admiration" (283); "His smiles came in succession like waves breaking on the surface of a little lake"(283); "smiling down on the top of her head" (283). As he did with Mrs. Hopewell, Pointer perseveres until he receives a response. He pulls a special look out of his bag of feigned expressions: he uses "his gaze of complete admiration" (283). He pretends to accept her ridiculous claim that she is "seventeen" (283). And he exaggerates his stupidity and inflates her vanity: "I think you're brave. I think you're real sweet" (283). Finally, his deceptiveness and persistence pay off; he hits a chink in Hulga's battleship armor when he tells her that he may die.

Hulga's voice and expression change. She has weighed all her previous answers; now she responds "suddenly" (283). She also "looked up at him" (283) and seems to respond to his eyes which "were very small and brown, glittering feverishly" (284)--although she still fails to read the danger in those eyes. He detects the change in her attitude and presses her for the picnic date, again using his body to full effect:

> "Couldn't we go on a pic-nic tomorrow? Say yes, Hulga," he said and gave her a dying look as if he felt his insides about to drop out of him. He had even seemed to sway slightly toward her (284).

She cannot resist. And she spends the night before her hot date reviewing the "profound implications" (283) and anticipating the triumph of a legless girl over a mindless man: "She had lain in bed imagining dialogues for them that were inane on the surface but that reached below to depths that no Bible salesman would be aware of" (283). Little does she realize that such smug intellectual superiority destines her to stumble badly. Little does she realize that Pointer has used his nonverbal skills to feed her natural pride.

Hulga's plans and expectations, however, go astray on the big day. Unsuitably dressed for a date and insufficiently equipped for a picnic ("she didn't take anything to eat" [283]), Hulga waits impatiently for Pointer. Here O'Connor makes use of the time code. Despite Hulga's self deception that she is in control, it is Hulga who "set off for the gate at exactly ten o'clock" (284). And it is Pointer who makes her wait (by being late for his date--he's hiding behind a bush) and gives her "the furious feeling that she had been tricked" (284). By manipulating time, he has asserted his control, a control he never relinquishes. This control can be seen all over his face as he continues "smiling down on her as if he could not stop" (285), and it can be detected in his stride as he "walked lightly by her side, bouncing on his toes" (285).

His first real touch, coupled with his first question, should have warned her: "Putting his hand easily on the small of her back, he asked softly, 'Where does your wooden leg join on?'" (285). He has hit another sore spot: "She turned an ugly red and glared at him" (285). Disarming her with an "abashed" (285) look and the mention of God, Pointer acts out the bumbling country boy. When Hulga denies the existence of God--her assertiveness being somewhat undercut by her "looking forward and walking fast" (285)--Pointer goes to his bag of nonverbal tricks again: "He exclaimed as if he were too astonished to say anything else" (285); "he was bouncing at her side, fanning with his hat" (285); "he remarked, watching her out of the corner of his eye" (285). O'Connor now places the unlikely couple at "the edge of the wood" (285), and Hulga enters a new world when Pointer gives her her first kiss.

Predictably, Hulga sees this momentous moment in the life of a thirty-two-year-old maiden merely as "an unexceptional experience and all a matter of the mind's control. Some people might enjoy drain water if they were told it was vodka" (287). The physical and mental setting seem perfect for the seduction she had planned. Just as she had imagined, they approach the storage barn with its "rusted top" (286). First, though, he helps her over roots and holds back "the long swaying blades of thorn vine" (286) for her. They come out on "a sunlit hillside" (286) which is "sprinkled with small pink weeds" (286). Although they are out of the woods, she isn't. The cool barn, with its sun-shafted hayloft, becomes the scene for a startling reversal and revelation for Hulga.

Once again she misses many preliminary warning signs. When "he gazed at her now as if the fantastic animal at the zoo had put its paw through the bars and given him a loving poke" (286), she misreads him, thinking "he looked as if he wanted to kiss her again . . ." (286). Pointer presents her with the chance to take the next step by underlining a question with a regulator: "'Ain't there somewheres we can sit down sometime?' he murmured, his voice softening toward the end of the sentence" (286). "Sometime" becomes now as they make "rapidly" (286) for the "somewheres": the barn. She demonstrates her physical prowess by climbing the ladder into the loft, having given him "a contemptuous look" (286) for doubting her climbing ability. O'Connor tells us that he stood watching Hulga, "apparently awestruck" (286). The stress seems on the "apparently."

Once the couple settles down in the loft, the scene progresses as Hulga had hoped. He "began methodically kissing her face, making little noises like a fish" (287). She doesn't seem to notice that he keeps his hat on (although "it was pushed far enough back not to interfere" [287]), or that he takes her glasses off. Eventually, she kisses him. He "mumbled" (287) that he loved her then makes his first demand on her: "You got to say you love me" (287). Instead of mumbling her own response, Hulga, proud that her mind had "never stopped or lost itself for a second to her feelings" (287), gives him a philosophical answer. "Frowning" (287), he repeats his demand. His apparent lack of comprehension causes Hulga to look at him "almost tenderly" (287) and to tell him patronizingly that he doesn't understand--never realizing her own lack of comprehension and understanding. His "astonished eyes looked blankly" (287) and "he almost whined" (287) his question again. His expressions, his tones of voice, and O'Connor's diction in this scene support Preston M.

Browning's contention that "actually Hulga longs for the warmth of human contact, longs in fact for a relationship in which she can play the dual roles of protected child and adoring mother."[29] Pointer's concern for her appeals to the former role, his apparent childishness to the latter. Just like a child who wants something, "The boy's look was irritated but dogged" (288).

And still the scene continues as Hulga had hoped. Mouthing that she wants no dishonesty between them, she admits her age to be thirty (still two years too young). Then Hulga feels triumphant when Pointer asks her to prove her love: "She smiled looking dreamily out on the shifty landscape. She had seduced him without even making up her mind to try" (288). The reversal comes when Pointer turns his attention not to her body, but to its appendage: her wooden leg. And she gives in to his outrageous demands.

Pointer orchestrates the submission both verbally and nonverbally. His request generates an immediate nonverbal response from Hulga as she "uttered a sharp little cry and her face instantly drained of color" (288). When she at first refuses to reveal her leg, he "muttered" (288) that she has been taking him "for a sucker" (288). She "cried" (288) out a question. And then they exchange visual signals. He gives her "a long penetrating look" (288) as he truthfully tells her that her leg makes her different. "She sat staring at him" (288) with her "round freezing blue eyes" (289). Yet again she fails to read his intentions correctly. Ignoring his eyes--and her own, she trusts her mind which tells her that she is "face to face with real innocence" (289).

When she submits, her tone--"a hoarse high voice" (289)--reveals what her face had hidden--"There was nothing about her face or her round freezing-blue eyes to indicate that this had moved her" (288-89). She is losing control. He is getting his way. His "face and his voice [are] entirely reverent" (289) as he plays with her leg, and he has "a delighted child's face" (289). Putting her leg aside, Pointer puts the moves on again. And in losing her leg, Hulga now loses the power of her mind--and her disturbance finally shows as "different expressions raced back and forth over her face" (289). Pointer's expression changes little; his eyes still penetrate "like two steel spikes" (289). He opens his Bible and lays out his perversion: whiskey, cards, and condoms. Innocence, indeed. Only now does Hulga drop her pretense as her voice takes on her mother's platitude: "'Aren't you,' she murmured, 'aren't you just good country people?'" (290). And only now does Pointer allow his face to show open contempt, "curling his lip slightly" (290). Their dialogue, their vocal tones, and their faces lose all pretense as the seduction disintegrates. He asks her "coaxingly" (290) to continue. But she "screamed" (290) her rejection; her face becomes "almost purple" (290); and "she hissed" (290) her accusation that he's an hypocritical Christian. This is too much for him, as his face and voice show: "The boy's mouth was set angrily. 'I hope you don't think,' he said in a lofty indignant tone, 'that I believe in that crap . . .'" (290). Had she bothered to look at him and to listen to him more perceptively, she would never have fallen into his trap. As he disappears, his final look "no longer had any admiration in it" (291).

Her final humiliation comes as Pointer leaves the loft with her leg: "'You ain't so smart. I been believing in nothing ever since I was born!'" (291). In a complete reversal of Hulga's dreams for the day, Pointer, having taken her physical shame away (the artificial leg), gives her a deeper understanding of life--but whether this revelation turns Hulga into someone useful remains one of O'Connor's untold tales. The chances seem good, though, that Hulga has learned something. By the time Pointer leaves, she has stopped pretending with her face and with her voice that her mind can comprehend everything--and nothing. Our final image of Hulga is a nonverbal one. She sits in the hayloft with a "churning face" (291). She has been shaken out of her complacency. There's hope for her.

But as the final paragraph makes clear, there's no hope for change in either Mrs. Freeman or Mrs. Hopewell. In O'Connor's fictional world, revelation comes painfully, even fatally. And yet the absence of revelation for other characters seems even more disturbing. In this story, for example, O'Connor emphasizes the persistence of the dangerously vapid majority by framing "Good Country People" with Mrs. Freeman and Mrs. Hopewell, two of her most formidable genotypes. They seem incapable of comprehending anything. Neither lady has been forced into the self-examination that Hulga experiences. Both ladies in their final words in the story show how wrong they can be. "Squinting" (291) as she watches Pointer disappear, Mrs. Hopewell sees only a "nice dull young man . . . so simple" (291) and suspects that he has been selling Bibles to "the Negroes" (291) rather than taking a leg from Hulga. Pulling an "evil-smelling onion shoot" from the "back pasture," Mrs. Freeman smugly refers to Pointer: "'Some can't be that simple,' she said. 'I know I never could'" (291).

In the story examined here, artifacts, physical appearance, body clues, and vocal tones all play critical roles. We should find ourselves much more perceptive than any of the characters concerning these clues. We may not know the exact, bizarre outcome of the seduction, but we should be aware that Pointer is fooling Hulga and that Hulga fools herself. We have indeed been prepared for the reversal which occurs. O'Connor also uses, to a limited extent, the time code (when Pointer arrives late), the touch code (the unromantic groping in the hayloft), the space code (from the house to the outside to the hayloft), and regulators.

Her use of regulators and vocal tones in this and other stories reinforces her belief that "you can't say anything meaningful about the mystery of a personality unless you put that personality in a believable and significant social context. And the best way to do this is through the character's own language."   In fact, she goes on to criticize stories that are empty of certain nonverbal features, stories in which the "characters have no distinctive speech to reveal themselves with; and sometimes they have no really distinctive features."[30]   And by language she meant much more than the words themselves.   She made her own characters come alive through a combination of their actions, their dialogue, and their nonverbal traits.

Throughout O'Connor's fiction, characters reveal themselves.   With the blatantly vacuous characters, such as her legion of southern farm ladies and helpers, most of the revelations come through the verbal.   Just as Mrs. Hopewell and Mrs. Freeman carry on empty conversations as they pull onion shoots, so do Mrs. Cope and Mrs. Pritchard ("A Circle in the Fire") as they pull weeds.   Readers listening to these cliche-ridden, often morbid dialogues hear O'Connor's message.   These characters are imprisoned within their own egocentric worlds, and the narrow boundaries of their self-imposed prisons are mapped out by their own inane utterances.

With O'Connor's more complex characters, however, readers have to go beyond the verbal for answers.   In Pointer, for example, she has created one of the most fascinating nonverbal characters in her--or any--fiction.   A number of her complex characters offer nonverbal clues about themselves--The Misfit, for instance, in "A Good Man Is Hard To Find," has an ominous adaptor habit: "The Misfit pointed the toe of his shoe into the ground and made a little hole and then covered it up again" (127).   But none of her characters seem so consciously aware and manipulative of the nonverbal as Pointer.   He reads the clues provided by others and controls the clues he offers himself. He is a classic con-man.

Another complex con-man in O'Connor further demonstrates the importance of a nonverbal approach to her work.   Mr. Shiftlet in "The Life You Save May Be Your Own" trades in his bachelorhood for a used car; once he has his car, he leaves his wife. But neither his trickery nor his manipulation of the nonverbal is nearly as successful as Pointer's. As Walters concludes, "Mr. Shiftlet, the 'shifty' deceiver, is above all self-deceived."[31] Unlike Pointer, Shiftlet lacks total control of his actions. He does play a number of roles (tramp, philosopher, restorer, teacher, husband, mentor, guide) to gain his ends, but, as Feeley demonstrates, he keeps "'trying on' roles and poses to hide his essential incompleteness."[32]

As he walks into the story in the first paragraph, his physical incompleteness sticks out: "His left coat sleeve was folded up to show there was only half an arm in it and his gaunt figure listed slightly to the side as if the breeze were pushing him" (145). In keeping with the nonverbal pattern in "Good Country People," O'Connor uses appearance in this story to capture the essential physical and psychological qualities and limitations of her major characters. With his "long black slick hair," "prominent forehead," and "jutting steel-trap jaw" (146-47), Shiftlet takes on "a look of composed dissatisfaction as if he understood life thoroughly" (146). Yet he doesn't. His play may be slick and smart enough to trap a country woman and her deaf mute daughter, but he is as psychologically mixed up near the end of the story as his clothing is at the beginning: "He had on a black town suit and brown felt hat . . ." (145).

The other characters in the story receive brief but suggestive descriptions. Color initially characterizes the daughter. She has "long pink-gold hair and eyes as blue as a peacock's neck" (146), a "big rosy" face (150), and wears "a short blue organdy dress" (145). And even though her outfit changes for her wedding ("a white dress . . . and . . . a Panama hat . . . with a bunch of red wooden cherries on the brim" [153]), nothing else does. Poor of sight and full of innocence when we first meet her, young Lucynell Crater gets abandoned at the Hot Spot with her eyes "half-shut" and her hair as "pink-gold" (154) as ever. The only softening of this harsh moment comes when "a pale youth with a greasy rag hung over his shoulder" went and "touched his finger to a strand of the golden hair . . ." (154-55). Significantly, this is the only time O'Connor uses the touch code in this story. The absence of touch reflects the absence of love.

Although the mother pays lip service to loving her daughter, she seems more interested in what a husband would bring to her farm than to her daughter. She may be "ravenous for a son-in-law" (150) because "she had no teeth" (146) and no way of putting "a new roof on her garden house" (148) without a man around. Indeed, she asks him what he carries in his tool box long before she asks him if he is married. She wears the "man's gray hat" (146) in the family, but things have deteriorated since her husband's death, in part, because she is only "the size of a cedar fence post" (146). Thus O'Connor uses a wooden image, as she did with Hulga, to describe both Mrs. Crater and Mr. Shiftlet, the carpenter, ("his figure formed a crooked cross" [146])--descriptions which suggest the woodenness of their souls.

The artifacts in the story, however, go beyond wood into metal. A rusted 1928 or 1929 Ford catches Shiftlet's eye. It becomes his bedroom and the object of his desire. With the help of a new fan belt, a little gasoline, and a lot of tinkering, he resurrects the car which had died with Mr. Crater fifteen years previously. The transformation gives him great pride: "He had an expression of serious modesty on his face as if he had just raised the dead" (151). The car offers him an escape, he hopes, from both himself and from the Crater world. Hendin contends that "his loathing of his own body is so great that he can love only a machine. . . ."[33] This love of the car drives him to an unsatisfactory wedding ("something a woman in an office did, nothing but paper work and blood tests" [153]) and an unsatisfactory encounter with a runaway. A wanderer by nature, Shiftlet finds his wanderlust accelerated by his dark green car with a yellow band around it. Even his destination at the end of the story--revealed in the last word, "Mobile" (156)--suggests more motion.

This mechanical motion occurs before a backdrop of an unforgiving and sometimes distorted natural environment. A "piercing sunset" (145) throws light on the opening of the story, but Shiftlet sees an illusion: "The sun . . . appeared to be balancing itself on the peak of a small mountain" (145). When the sun disappears, it is replaced by a "fat yellow moon" which "appeared in the branches of the fig tree as if it were going to roost there with the chickens" (148). Like the sun, the moon also "visited" the three black mountains which stood out "against the dark blue sky" (150). Both sun and moon are also on the move, although with more predictability than Shiftlet.

Another piercing, distorted, and moving sunset throws light on the climax of the story. "The sun began to set directly in front of the automobile. It was a reddening ball that through his windshield was slightly flat on the bottom and top" (155). O'Connor makes full use of the elements to dramatize the scene. A storm brews, "preparing very slowly and without thunder as if it meant to drain every drop of air from the earth before it broke" (155). The road is as "narrow" and the fields are as "dry" (155) as is his life. This fictional world seems to Hendin to be "withered universe. . . . Everyone in it is in some way warped or deformed; its air is thick and so dusty that clouds grow in it like turnips."[34] And these clouds force Shiftlet to drive his machine even faster in an attempt to avoid nature's retribution.

By focusing on artifacts, especially in the final scene, readers can see Shiftlet's disturbance--a disturbance Pointer never seems to have felt. Warned earlier by signs that "The life you save may be your own" (155), Shiftlet comes to this fearful realization after "a boy in overalls and a gray hat" (155) rejects and abandons him, just as Shiftlet has abandoned his own mother and wife. A cloud, the color of the boy's hat and the shape of a turnip, descends on him and makes him pray. In his fear, he hears nature laugh at him ("guffawing peal of thunder" [156]) and his own metal god mocked ("raindrops, like tin-can tops" [156]). His response holds little promise of any change: "Very quickly he stepped on the gas and with his stump sticking out the window he raced the galloping shower into Mobile" (156). O'Connor's artifacts, then, serve to underline Shiftlet's distorted vision of nature and his distorted value for machines. The artifacts externalize the internal.

Body clues and vocal tones, however, tend to show readers that Shiftlet has shady motives. His first pose--turning his back and forming a cross--has little impact on Mrs. Crater: she "watched him with her arms folded across her chest . . ."(146). He speaks in "a firm nasal voice" (146) and looks with a "pale sharp glance" (146). Once he spots the car, he goes to work with his voice and body, manipulating them for a while in good Pointer style. When he tells her about a surgeon removing someone's heart, he dramatizes his story by repeating a line, "leaning forward", and then "allowing a long significant pause in which his head slid forward and his clay-colored eyes brightened . . . (147). Unlike Pointer, however, he cannot consistently control his face; he gives himself away to readers and, to a certain extent, to Mrs. Crater with his "sly look" (147).

When she offers him a job in return for a place to sleep, though, he removes his sly look and replaces it with "no particular expression" (148). Furthermore, he tries to regulate the pace of his dialogue--"he said slowly" (148)--to add sincerity to his voice. But a telling body clue of his anxiety and duplicity, which O'Connor emphasizes, in part, by showing it through the daughter's eyes, gives him away again: "The daughter watched the trigger that moved up and down his neck" (148). O'Connor further emphasizes the body clue as opposed to the words themselves by using indirect dialogue when he tells his life story, just as she had for Pointer's autobiography. When she does revert to direct dialogue, Shiftlet again tries to use regulation to impress Mrs. Crater. She asks him if he is married; his answer "finally" follows "a long silence" (149). Despite his efforts, though, he fails to trick her nonverbally; he really never impresses Mrs. Crater. She tolerates him because they are involved in trying to fool one another.

He tries to deceive her by speaking "kindly" (149) about the daughter and seeks to impress her by claiming he had "a moral intelligence!" (149); he underlines this claim with his eyes as "he stared at her as if he were astonished himself at this impossible truth" (149). Once again, O'Connor helps readers, this time with the words "as if"; these words show the falseness of his body clue. Whereas such help really helps with a character like Pointer who fools Mrs. Hopewell and Hulga consistently, it does not take on such importance with a lesser con-man like Shiftlet who doesn't even fully fool Mrs. Crater: she "was not impressed with the phrase" (149). Nor does Mrs. Crater fool Shiftlet. When she asks him to teach Lucynell the word "sugarpie," she gives herself away with a smile that "was broad and toothless and suggestive" (150). O'Connor lets us know quite simply that "Mr. Shiftlet already knew what was on her mind" (151).

They continue to spar, though, as she seeks a son-in-law and a handy-man for her farm and as he seeks a honeymoon and a paint job for his beloved car. When she offers her daughter, she does it "sympathetically" (151); when he asks for money, he does it "firmly" (152). His request for money for a honeymoon is at first met with a "muttered" (152) response and later with "a crabbed voice" (153). His request for money for a paint job meets with more success as "she laid the bait carefully" (152) by agreeing. Once again, he cannot control his true face when he triumphs: "Mr. Shiftlet's smile stretched like a weary snake waking up by a fire" (152). And once again, he hides his true face following this short lapse: "After a second he recalled himself . . ." (152). Throughout the story, O'Connor relies on readers to spot such nonverbal oscillations. Sometimes, as with this telling smile, only readers become privy to his duplicity, since some of his body clues occur "in the darkness" (152).

He, however, does not hide his displeasure with the marriage ceremony: "Mr. Shiftlet began twisting his neck in his collar. He looked morose and bitter . . ." (153). Not only does he dislike the ceremony, but he also displays an insensitivity to his bride and his mother-in-law. O'Connor confirms this insensitivity with two stylistically parallel simple sentences. When Mrs. Crater says that Lucynell looks pretty, "Mr. Shiftlet didn't even look at her" (153). When Mr. Crater cries at their departure, "Mr. Shiftlet started the motor" (154). He no longer needs his contrived looks and tones. He has his car.

But he also has Lucynell. The "aluminum-painted eating place called The Hot Spot" (154) provides him with an opportunity to desert her. Even though the serving boy "looked up and stared" at him and "murmured" that "'She looks like an angel of Gawd'" (154), Mr. Shiftlet shows no compassion. Lying twice to the boy--"'Hitchhiker,' Mr. Shiftlet explained. 'I can't wait. I got to make Tuscaloosa'" (155)--he leaves her asleep on the counter. Yet his depression deepens. The runaway boy standing by the roadside seems to offer him some chance of atonement, some chance to save a life. However, the boy rejects him both verbally and nonverbally.

At first, he rejects Mr. Shiftlet's initial attempt at talk when "he turned his head and looked out the window away from Mr. Shiftlet" (155). Mr. Shiftlet's next verbal attempt receives another nonverbal answer: "The boy gave him a quick dark glance and then turned his face back out the window" (155). As Mr. Shiftlet starts talking about his own mother, "The boy shifted in his seat but he didn't look at Mr. Shiftlet" (156). As with Ole in Hemingway's "The Killers," the boy's avoidance of eye contact seriously disturbs his companion; it is a devastating nonverbal message. It leads Mr. Shiftlet into talking, for the first time in the story, in a "very strained voice" (156); it brings tears to his eyes; and it slows down his driving. And in an interesting parallel to Hulga's breaking into her mother's dialogue under stress, Mr. Shiftlet picks up the phraseology of The Hot Spot boy: "My mother was a Angel of Gawd" (156). This hypocrisy is too much for his passenger who jumps out of the car, having "cried" out his one message: "You go to the devil! . . . . My old woman is a flea bag and yours is a stinking pole cat! (156). Shiftlet has met up with the truth. He, too, has been rejected.

Whether he recognizes that truth and changes as a result of it seems ambiguous. Hendin believes "Shiftlet is restored,"[35] whereas Walters feels "his own spiritual life is in imminent danger."[36] His cry for the Lord to "Break forth and wash the slime from this earth" (155) offers some hope for his restoration. But when the rain comes to do just that, his blindness seems to return. Instead of waiting to be cleansed, he races to avoid the rain. His action speaks louder than his words.

In this story, O'Connor has followed a similar nonverbal pattern to the one she designed in "Good Country People." She uses artifacts, physical appearance, vocal tones, and body clues, in part, to contribute to our understanding of her characters. By contrasting these elements, for example, in Pointer and Shiftlet, we can see that although they are both depraved con-men, they are actually quite different and perform quite differently functions for O'Connor. Shiftlet's words have nearly as much credibility as Pointer's. But Pointer and Shiftlet are worlds apart nonverbally. Pointer, who functions as a foil to and of Hulga, never loses control of his voice or

his body until he has Hulga completely fooled, and readers have to rely
heavily on O'Connor to know when he is manipulating. Not so with Shiftlet.
He may be able to manipulate his voice--"he . . . paused and made his tone
more ominous still" (148)--but he doesn't completely fool anyone but himself.
As Browning puts it: "Shiftlet is an especially interesting psychological
type because . . . he himself is taken in by the pious cant which is his
hallmark. Manley Pointer is a scoundrel and knows it; Pointer . . . revels in
his knavery. Shiftlet is a victim of his own rhetoric. The person he cons
most consistently is himself."[37] In one sense, Shiftlet is an amalgamation of
Pointer and Hulga. Functioning as the protagonist, he deceives himself as
does Hulga, and he also becomes the unsuspecting victim at the end.

A nonverbal approach to O'Connor helps keep such endings in perspective.
Not surprisingly, readers tend to remember the shocking climaxes of her
stories. Hulga loses her wooden leg; Shiftlet drives with his arm stump out
of the window; others lose their lives (by mass murder, by suicide, by bull
goring, by accident). And, as O'Connor intended, readers search for meaning
in these episodes--episodes in which O'Connor particularly shouts to the hard
of hearing and draws startling pictures for the blind. It is her endings that
put the greatest strain on credulity. It is her endings that so often
encourage a one-dimensional critical attitude toward her work.

All too often readers and critics tend to forget what has come before,
what has prepared us for these endings. Writing for what she assumes will be
an unbelieving and unseeing audience, O'Connor initially captures her readers
with the familiar and concrete before shocking them with the extraordinary and
abstract. And many of the familiar and concrete details seem to be nonverbal
ones because these details so often reveal characters succinctly and
realistically; these details, then, function as her "convincing . . .
properties," as part of her "fictional manipulation."[38] Readers should

144

recognize, with O'Connor's help, that an understanding of nonverbal behavior can be especially important in uncovering the hypocrisy that she sees all around us. That fervor against hypocrisy--seeing hypocrisy as a human as well as a divine failing--leads to a precarious balance in her fiction. She places the weight on realism, the force on surrealism. The audience sensitive to the nonverbal and undiverted by maps of the South, Catholic doctrines, and cosmic scriptures profits from both the weight and force. And understands.

Notes

[1] In a letter "To John Hawkes," 28 November 1961, in *The Habit of Being*, ed. Sally Fitzgerald (New York: Farrar, Straus and Giroux, 1979), p. 457, she notes:

> I think I would admit to writing what Hawthorne called
> 'romances,' but I don't think that has anything to do with
> the romantic mentality. Hawthorne interests me consider-
> ably. I feel more of a kinship with him than with any
> other American.

Others spotted the kinship, too. See, especially, Leon V. Driskell and Joan T. Brittain, *The Eternal Crossroads: The Art of Flannery O'Connor* (Lexington: The Univ. Press of Kentucky, 1971), pp. 14-32.

[2] See, in particular, "The Church and the Fiction Writer," "Novelist and Believer," "Catholic Novelists and Their Readers," "The Catholic Novelist in the Protestant South," *Mystery and Manners*, ed. Sally and Robert Fitzgerald (New York: Farrar, Straus and Giroux, 1957), pp. 143-209.

[3] A review of titles on O'Connor reveals these preoccupations. See, for example, Gilbert H. Muller, *Nightmares and Visions: Flannery O'Connor and the Catholic Grotesque* (Athens: Univ. of Georgia Press, 1972); David Eggenschwiler, *The Christian Humanism of Flannery O'Connor* (Detroit: Wayne State Univ. Press, 1972); and Robert Coles, *Flannery O'Connor's South* (Baton Rouge: Louisiana State Univ. Press, 1980).

[4] Melvin J. Friedman, in his introduction to the collection of essays, *The Added Dimension: The Art and Mind of Flannery O'Connor*, ed. Melvin J. Friedman and Lewis A. Lawson (New York: Fordham Univ. Press, 1966), p. 11.

[5] O'Connor, *Mystery and Manners*, p. 97.

[6] O'Connor, *Mystery and Manners*, pp. 67, 103, 104, respectively.

[7] Friedman, p. 205.

[8] Friedman, p. 199.

[9] O'Connor, *Mystery and Manners*, p. 70.

[10] Sister Kathleen Feeley, *Flannery O'Connor: Voice of the Peacock* (New Brunswick, N.J.: Rutgers Univ. Press, 1972), p. 22.

[11] Friedman, p. 17.

[12] Flannery O'Connor, "Good Country People," in *The Complete Stories* (New York: Farrar, Straus and Giroux, 1975), p. 275. All further references to O'Connor's short stories will be taken from this edition and will be included in the text.

[13] Josephine Hendin, *The World of Flannery O'Connor* (Bloomington: Indiana Univ. Press, 1970), p. 72.

[14] Eggenschwiler, p. 12.

[15] O'Connor, *Mystery and Manners*, p. 99.

[16] Dorothy Walters, *Flannery O'Connor*, Twayne United States Authors Series, ed. Sylvia E. Bowman (Boston: Twayne Publishers, 1973), p. 67.

[17] Dorothy Tuck McFarland, *Flannery O'Connor* (New York: Frederick Ungar Publishing, 1976), p. 40.

[18] Eggenschwiler, p. 57.

[19] Walters, p. 66.

[20] Walters, p. 147.

[21] McFarland, p. 40.

[22] Also, see the Misfit's removing and cleaning of his glasses at the end of "A Good Man Is Hard To Find." See Stephen R. Portch, "A Good Man Is Hard To Find," *The Explicator*, 37, No. 1 (1978), 19-20.

[23] Hendin, p. 29.

[24] O'Connor had a fascination for cars. Her letters (see pp. 148, 288, 291, 504, 523, 534, and 535) reveal her own ineptitude with cars. Her stories frequently show how cars (and buses and trains) convey mobility and new spacial dimensions. See especially "The Life You Save May Be Your Own."

[25] Martha Stephens, *The Question of Flannery O'Connor* (Baton Rouge: Louisiana State Univ. Press, 1973), pp. 9-10.

[26] Walters, p. 27.

[27] For a discussion of build and personality see J. B. Cortes and F. M. Gatti, "Physique and Propensity," *Psychology Today*, 4 (1970), 84. For a discussion of color and meaning see Burgoon and Saine, p. 110. In their table,

"Color in the Environment: Moods Created and Symbolic Meanings," blue equates with truth and yellow with wisdom.

[28] Michael Argyle and Mark Cook, *Gaze and Mutual Gaze* (Cambridge: Cambridge Univ. Press, 1976), pp. 92-93.

[29] Preston M. Browning, Jr., *Flannery O'Connor*, Crosscurrents Modern Critiques Series, ed. Harry T. Moore (Carbondale: Southern Illinois Univ. Press, 1974), p. 47. For examples of O'Connor's diction, see: "His breath was clear and sweet like a child's and the kisses were sticky like a child's. . . . The mumbling was like the sleeping fretting of a child being put to sleep by his mother" (287). Also, she calls him a "poor baby" (287).

[30] *Mystery and Manners*, p. 104-05.

[31] Walters, p. 83.

[32] See Feeley, pp. 28-29.

[33] Hendin, p. 68.

[34] Hendin, p. 64.

[35] Hendin, p. 69.

[36] Walters, p. 84.

[37] Preston M. Browning, Jr., *Flannery O'Connor*, Crosscurrents, Modern Critique Series, ed. Harry T. Moore (Carbondale: Southern Illinois Univ. Press, 1974), p. 60.

[38] Carol Schloss, *Flannery O'Connor's Dark Comedies*, Southern Literary Studies Series, ed. Louis D. Rubin, Jr. (Baton Rouge: Louisiana State Univ. Press, 1980), p. 125.

Chapter 6
CONCLUSION

"What does a fish know about the water in which he swims all his life?"

Albert Einstein in *Out of My Later Years*.

Einstein's fish has experienced but not fully understood the water in which it swims. So, too, with our relationship to the nonverbal elements in our lives and in our literature. An awareness of the presence of nonverbal communication exists; an understanding of that existence is often incomplete--with nonverbal sensitivities varying from person to person. Indeed, Joel Davitz and his research colleagues concede that "Individuals differ in their ability to communicate," but they conclude that "notwithstanding these individual differences, our results demonstrate incontrovertibly that nonverbal, emotional communication is a stable, measurable phenomenon."[1] But how can it be measured in fiction?

First, we have to recognize that authors themselves differ in their ability to communicate meaning, at least partially, through nonverbal elements. The three authors studied here seem to have mastered many of the possibilities. Others mentioned in passing (particularly Twain and James) or as examples also appear to have been alert to some of the potential of nonverbal communication. Their awareness, however, probably occurs because of the perceptiveness of human behavior demanded by their art form. Only occasionally do we find any reference by an author to the research or to the specialized language used by those who study nonverbal behavior. We can certainly speculate that as the research in the field becomes more generally known and widely accepted that authors will perhaps become more conscious of the potential of nonverbal communication to function as a specific technique in their work. Such consciousness, however, might well be detrimental to their art--especially if some authors begin to use any of the excessive jargon that goes with so much of the research. The research simply labels what all good writers have always known.

Second, we have to acknowledge that despite our everyday exposure to, and involvement in, nonverbal communication, few readers have stopped to study the phenomenon. Many readers in this century, however, may well unknowingly have become more alert to nonverbal communication in literature as a consequence of the film medium. When the camera zooms in on a facial expression, the film audience cannot help but focus on its significance, on its meaning. It seems likely, then, that readers who create visual images from written words may recognize the importance of a described nonverbal moment in the written medium.

But this leaves a great deal to chance--the chance that readers will notice, the chance that readers will understand. As the nonverbal research consistently demonstrates, those who notice nonverbal behavior even in real life are inconsistent in their powers of observation and interpretation. By using a "system," however, that draws from existing nonverbal research and which demands very close attention to the text, readers can be assured of a higher level of observation and, perhaps, comprehension. The nine benchmarks in the system allow the separation--but not isolation--of several distinct nonverbal elements. These elements must not be isolated because they have an inter-relationship. Distinct though they may seem, an author's use of space and body clues, for example, may be related: are, for instance, the characters close enough to detect all the body clues? Perhaps the most consistent relationship between two elements occurs between vocal tones and body clues. In each of the three authors examined, this proved to be true. Indeed, with an author like Hemingway who uses so few adverbs or adjectives to describe vocal tones, the relationship becomes a critical one. For the body expresses the voice.

By studying in detail a few works by three authors, several patterns emerge. All three authors use all nine nonverbal elements, but to varying degrees. Hawthorne favors vocal tones, body clues, physical appearance, and artifacts; he also frequently regulates dialogue with questions. So, too, does Hemingway. And Hemingway prefers vocal tones, body clues, time, artifacts, and physical appearance. O'Connor inclines to artifacts, physical appearance, body clues, and vocal tones. Such knowledge about these authors' nonverbal preferences, interesting though it may be, does not alone justify this approach to their works. What justifies it, is what's added to our ability to read and to comprehend their fiction.

A nonverbal approach adds to our sensitivity and perceptivity. Any approach that forces readers to respond to the total effect of the unspoken sheds new light on the fiction. Hemingway's fictional world, for example, has been called "a world made up of fragments of sensation that are linear in their progression and cumulative in their intensity."[2] So many of these fragments are nonverbal, so much of his fiction is "purely behavioristic narrative."[3] In a story like "The Killers," a nonverbal approach enables us to fill a significant gap in previous criticism of the story: the role of the gangsters. Their nonverbal behavior confirms that they are dangerously inexperienced rather than true professionals. Such an interpretation is consistent with the theme of the story--that Nick will be scarred by fear. It also explains why the gangsters have such a presence in the story and why they behave as illogically and irrationally as they so often do. If all the nonverbal fragments had not been pieced together, the riddle would have remained.

A nonverbal approach also adds to our ability to solve cases of ambiguity. All three authors delight in ambiguity, in forcing the reader to make choices. William Empson, in *Seven Types of Ambiguity*, suggests that we call a work "ambiguous . . . when we recognize that there could be a puzzle as to what the author meant, in that alternative views might be taken without sheer misreading."[4] Each of the stories examined could thus be termed "ambiguous." Is Robin changed? Does Young Goodman Brown dream the whole scene? Is Nick deeply affected by the gangsters' actions and Ole's inactions? Will the girl have an abortion? Will Hulga change because of losing her leg? Will Shiftlet outrace the rain? These are fundamental questions without certain answers. But in each case, nonverbal details provide critical clues. In Robin's trial, for example, vocal tones tell much of the tale. And by establishing a pattern of tones for the naive Robin, Hawthorne creates a signal by breaking the pattern. When Robin speaks "dryly" at the end of the story, his tone tips us off to his increasing maturity more than the words he speaks. Some ambiguity in such stories remains, but readers who have noted nonverbal clues throughout the story can have greater assurance that they possess supportable solutions to the puzzles deliberately presented.

A nonverbal approach can further add to our concept of the development of the short story genre. This minimal sampling of stories from Hawthorne to Hemingway to O'Connor begins to reveal continuity and change. The continuity seems to be in theme; the change occurs in its execution. All the stories studied here in some way revolve around the themes of maturation and initiation. Such themes have long been the province of the short story because they enable the author to take a relatively long process and dramatize and symbolize it through an abbreviated conflict. O'Connor in particular specializes in this dramatized moment which takes on the force of revelation. A key element in the maturation and initiation themes is the almost inevitable disorientation that occurs during such a traumatic process. And the nonverbal technique provides a perfect mechanism for revealing disorientation. Robin loses his sense of time, space, and artifacts; Nick survives in a world where time and behavior seem strangely out of synchronization; Hulga cannot see clearly out of the hayloft. The ironies persist as expectations dissolve. But so often these are dramatic ironies, for authors like O'Connor help readers distinguish between a character's deceptive and truthful nonverbal moments--a distinction not always apparent to other characters in the story.

Beyond the themes, however, change can be seen in style through a nonverbal approach. Any approach, even the most casual reading, would spot that Hemingway is no Hawthorne: the former has stripped his prose to a skeleton. Nowhere is the difference more dramatic than in describing vocal tones. Hawthorne insists not only on aiding readers with adjectives and adverbs, but also on choosing descriptive verbs (for example, "shouted"); Hemingway either uses the barest of verbs (for example, "said") or nothing at all. Linguists are beginning to study the syntactical differences between the verbs which denote nonverbal communication and those which seem to be neutral about the behavior which accompanies the words themselves.[5] Bronislaw Malinowski, however, offers some sound advice to such linguists: "It is very profitable in linguistics to widen the concept of context so that it embraces not only spoken words but facial expression, gesture, bodily activities . . . and the part of the environment on which . . . people are engaged."[6] Hemingway provides the perfect example of what Malinowski means. What Hemingway accomplished was a verbal neutrality charged with nonverbal meaning. From the total context of the story and the rhythms of the dialogue, we can hear the tones of voice without ever having them described. That's style and meaning.

Because of the stylistic influence of both Hawthorne and Hemingway on the writers following them, any approach which adds insight into any element of their styles has value.

A further value from a nonverbal approach for those interested in style comes with an author like O'Connor. For this approach forces readers into an initial minute examination of the text (perhaps into nine distinct readings of the text) and not into early considerations of external religious or geographical influences on the author. Such an examination of an O'Connor text reveals that she is a stylist of the first order. Again, vocal tones provide an example: she has a mastery of which dialogues to record and which to report. Sometimes, as in the exchange below between the grandmother and June Star in "A Good Man Is Hard To Find," she achieves a devastating, ironic understatement:

> "She wouldn't stay at home for a million bucks," June Star said. "Afraid she'd miss something. She has to go everywhere we go."
> "All right, Miss," the grandmother said. "Just remember that the next time you want me to curl your hair."
> June Star said her hair was naturally curly (118).

Yet not a single critic has drawn attention to this technique. If readers need to find a link between O'Connor's fiction and the ecumenical spirit of the Second Vatican Council, they can find a suitable article.[7] But if readers need to probe the niceties of her style, they will find a vacuum in the criticism. And although a nonverbal reading does not concentrate on style alone, it does focus on the fiction itself.

Because of the minute examination involved when noticing, combining, and understanding the nonverbal elements, the short story proves the most suitable genre for such an approach. The short story needs the nonverbal more than the novel does. Brevity demands that characters be created and captured through essential characteristics, which include the nonverbal. That flash of recognition and understanding from readers can come from noticing the smallest of details about a character. Although an awareness of the nonverbal does enrich reading a novel and watching a play, the cataloguing of each nonverbal event would, in many cases, be a mammoth task; and the resulting information would often be beyond synthesis. That may explain why a recent and important book, Fernando Poyatos's *New Perspectives in Nonverbal Communication*, that includes chapters on "Nonverbal Communication in the Novel: the Author-Character-Reader Relationship" and "Nonverbal Communication in the Theater: the Playright-Actor-Spectator Relationship," does not attempt a demonstration of a systematic nonverbal approach in either of these genres. Yet Poyatos misses an opportunity to support his fascinating theories through the use of the short story.

Poyatos does, however, offer critical insights, pose important questions, and provide a complex system for comprehending the role of nonverbal communication in the novel and in the theatre. As he points out, communication gaps always exist between author and readers and from playwright to actor to audience. Writers create cultural and temporal settings that may well be foreign or unfamiliar to their audiences. Thus when readers get involved in "the creative-recreative multiple process"[8] of bringing characters to life, it in one sense results in the birth of new characters. The more adept readers are in bridging the cultural and temporal gaps, the closer that birth becomes instead a rebirth. What can make them more adept is a recognition of the nonverbal elements.

This recognition, Poyatos suggests, has been restricted because of "the limitations of written-typographical presentation of verbal behavior to portray vividly the physical and psychological configuration of . . . characters."[9] This need not be the case. He believes that authors should have available to them more methods for making their characters' nonverbal behavior clearer to readers. His suggestions include the greater use of paralanguage (such as "Ssh," "Hm," "Grr," and so on), the invention of new punctuation marks (such as an inverted question mark), and the creation of a kinealphabet (such as an alphabet signifying various body clues). To a certain extent, some of his suggestions have already begun to occur (for instance, the increased use of dashes and ellipsis to indicate pauses), but the likelihood of a dramatic change in the way authors communicate the nonverbal element in their characters seems remote. Therefore, critics and teachers of literature face the challenge of helping to close the cultural, temporal, and nonverbal gaps that stand between authors and readers.

Critics and teachers must develop the skills to recognize the subtlety that often surrounds an author's use of the nonverbal. Even an astute reader like Poyatos can miss the point. He correctly claims that Dickens and Steinbeck make vivid use of the nonverbal, but he errs in suggesting that Faulkner and Hemingway have no real interest in the nonverbal. As we have seen, for example, Hemingway's use may not be as apparent or as flambuoyant as Dickens', but it is every bit as important to his art and to his meaning. For that matter, the medium of nonverbal communication itself often operates in rather quiet ways, so its subtle use in literature comes all the closer to verisimilitude.

Indeed Poyatos himself insists that nonverbal communication in literature can become documentary evidence for the study of life itself by other disciplines. In a chapter entitled "Literary Anthropology: A New Interdisciplinary Perspective of Man Through His Narrative Literature," he suggests that literature may provide a perfect tool for cross-cultural studies throughout history by providing complementary insights to field studies. This is possible because "Narrative literature . . . constitutes without doubt the richest source of documentation of human life styles, as well as the most advance form of one's projection in time and space and of communicating with contemporary and future generations."[10] To visualize the environment of nineteenth century England, for instance, one can do no better than to read the great novels of the time, noting artifacts and their relationship to the other nonverbal codes and signs. On a smaller scale, contemporary regional differences can be detected by reading regional writers and noting distinctions in everything from vocal tones to clothes and cosmetics.

To make such observations of various cultures, "The researcher should seek the most systematic and exhaustive"[11] system to study nonverbal behaviors. The same holds true for literary observation and analysis. Such an approach has, admittedly, its limitations. The nine neat divisions suggested can never be quite that neat. The jargon can be distracting (two of the terms, "affect displays" and "vocalics," were changed for that reason). The line between nonverbal elements and traditional symbolism is often not a clear-cut one. Yet without the classifications and codes and without research from other disciplines, no new dimensions can be added to our reading and understanding of fiction and human behavior.

Many other possibilities exist within and beyond the use of the nonverbal made here. Although some attention has been given to the development of the short story genre, much still remains to be learned. A comprehensive examination from a nonverbal perspective of many works of many authors should add to our knowledge of developments in both theme and style. Beyond the scope of this study exists a fascinating possibility of examining cross-cultural distinctions in literature from a nonverbal perspective. For instance, the research shows that cultures differ in nonverbal as well as verbal language.

An exploration of nonverbal elements in the fiction of two or more cultures could provide evidence in the debate over the extent that nonverbal behavior is learned behavior. Such an exploration would be revealing both of physical differences (such as facial signals of emotions) and psychological concepts (such as attitudes towards time). It could involve both subcultures within one country (such as different geographic or ethnic units) and cultures between countries.

Another area worth attention is the difference in nonverbal behavior between the sexes. Although some research has been conducted on such differences by those interested in nonverbal communication (for example, in body clues of emotion), much remains to be done. Fiction could provide an interesting angle. Do male authors unwittingly give female characters male nonverbal behavior--and vice versa? Are those authors who receive acclaim for their accurate portrayal of the opposite sex, receiving such recognition, in part, for their sensitivity to differences in the nonverbal behavior of the sexes? In both the cultural and sex differences, examples from fiction may present nonverbal researchers with some of their most concrete material.

From a purely literary standpoint, the nonverbal approach has further possibilities. As with other elements of fiction, a review of an individual author's development could include attention to the use of the nonverbal. When a change occurs in a pattern--as with Hawthorne's change from extensive physical appearance description in "My Kinsman, Major Molineux" to a relative dearth in "Young Goodman Brown"--it may simply indicate a significance within the particular story, especially since these two stories were written within three years of one another. But when the stories come from more distinct phases of an author's career, such changes in nonverbal patterns may have a significance within that author's overall development.

Such an approach will not lead to a major revolution in the reading of literature nor will it result in a complete re-evaluation of the short story genre. But it will give readers of literature a most valuable mechanism for piecing together many of the mysteries unsolved by attention to dialogue and action alone. The author, Kenneth Burke tells us, "knows that 'shame' . . . is not merely a 'state,' but a movement of the eye, a color of the cheek, a certain quality of voice and set of the muscles; he knows this as 'behavioristically' as the formal scientific behaviorist. . . ."[12] The reader also needs to be able to make that connection between art and science--to recognize that minor movements can indeed be major moments in the American short story.

Notes

[1] Joel R. Davitz, et. al., *The Communication of Emotional Meaning* (New York: McGraw-Hill, 1964), p. 178.

[2] Eusebio L. Rodriques, "'Hills Like White Elephants': An Analysis," *Literary Criterion*, 5 (1962), 106.

[3] Kenneth Burke, *A Grammar of Motives* (Berkeley: Univ. of California Press, 1969), p. 274.

[4] William Empson, *Seven Types of Ambiguity*, 3rd ed. (New York: World Publishing, 1955), p. x.

[5] See, for example, John Robert Ross, "On Declarative Sentences," in Roderick A. Jacobs and Peter S. Rosenbaum, eds., *Readings in English Transformational Grammar* (Boston: Ginn, 1970), pp. 222-72. For a summary, see Mary Ritchie Key, *Paralanguage and Kinesics* (Metuchen, N.J.: The Scarecrow Press, 1975), pp. 39-40.

[6] As quoted in Key, p. 124.

[7] See Sister Mariella Gable, "Ecumenic Core in Flannery O'Connor's Fiction," *The American Benedictine Review*, 15 (1964), 127-43.

[8] Fernando Poyatos, *New Perspective in Nonverbal Communication: Studies in Cultural Anthropology, Social Psychology, Linguistics, Literature, and Semiotics* (Oxford: Pergamon, 1983), p. 295.

SELECTED BIBLIOGRAPHY

Primary Sources

Auden, W. H. "Thanksgiving for a Habitat." In *W. H. Auden Collected Poems*.
   Ed. Edward Mendelson. New York: Random House, 1976, pp. 518-39.
Bolt, Robert. *A Man For All Seasons*. New York: Random House, 1962.
Cather, Willa. "Paul's Case." In *Youth and the Bright Medusa*. New York:
   Alfred A. Knopf, 1920, pp. 199-234.
Chaucer, Geoffrey. *The Canterbury Tales*. In *The Works of Geoffrey Chaucer*.
   Ed. F. N. Robinson. 2nd ed. Boston: Houghton Mifflin, 1957, pp.
   17-265.
Crane, Stephen. *Maggie: A Girl of the Streets*. In *Bowery Tales*. Ed.
   Fredson Bowers. Charlottesville: The Univ. Press of Virginia, 1969, pp.
   7-77.
Fitzgerald, Sally, ed. *The Habit of Being: Letters of Flannery O'Connor*.
   New York: Farrar, Straus and Giroux, 1979.
Hawthorne, Nathaniel. "The Haunted Mind." In *Twice-Told Tales*. The
   Centenary Edition of the Works of Nathaniel Hawthorne. Vol. 9. Ed.
   William Charvat, Roy Harvey Pearce, and Claude M. Simpson. Columbus:
   Ohio State Univ. Press, 1974.
----------. "My Kinsman, Major Molineux." In *The Snow Images and Uncollected
   Tales*. The Centenary Edition of the Works of Nathaniel Hawthorne. Vol.
   11.
----------. "Young Goodman Brown," In *Mosses from an Old Manse*. The
   Centenary Edition of the Works of Nathaniel Hawthorne. Vol. 10.
Heller, Joseph. *Catch-22*. New York: Simon and Schuster, 1955.
Hemingway, Ernest. *A Moveable Feast*. New York: Charles Scribner's Sons,
   1964.
----------. *The Short Stories of Ernest Hemingway*. New York: Charles
   Scribner's Sons, 1938.
Mailer, Norman. *An American Dream*. New York: The Dial Press, 1965.
O'Connor, Flannery. *The Complete Stories*. New York: Farrar, Straus and
   Giroux, 1975.
----------. *Mystery and Manners*. Ed. Sally and Robert Fitzgerald. New York:
   Farrar, Straus and Giroux, 1957.
Roth, Philip. "Defender of the Faith." In *Goodbye Columbus and Five Short
   Stories*. Boston: Houghton Mifflin, 1959, pp. 161-200.
Salinger, J. D. "For Esme--With Love and Squalor." In *Nine Stories*. Boston:
   Little, Brown, 1948, pp. 131-73.
Smith, Lillian. *Strange Fruit*. New York: Reynal, 1944.
Steinbeck, John. *East of Eden*. New York: The Viking Press, 1952.
Stoppard, Tom. *Professional Foul*. In *Every Good Boy Deserves Favor and
   Professional Foul*. New York: Grove Press, 1978.
Thoreau, Henry David. *Walden*. Ed. J. Lyndon Shanley. Princeton, N. J.:
   Princeton Univ. Press, 1971.
Twain, Mark. *A Connecticut Yankee in King Arthur's Court*. New York: The New

American Library, 1963.
----------. *Adventures of Huckleberry Finn*. New York: Harper and Bros., 1923.
Updike, John. "A & P." In *Pigeon Feathers and Other Stories*. New York: Alfred A. Knopf, 1969, pp. 187-96.
----------. *Couples*. New York: Alfred A. Knopf, 1968.
----------. *Rabbit, Run*. New York: Alfred A. Knopf, 1960.

Secondary Sources

Adams, Richard P. "Sunrise Out of the Waste Land." *Tulane Studies in English*, 9 (1959), 119-31. Rpt. in Wagner, pp. 21-38.
Allen, Mary. "Smiles and Laughter in Hawthorne." *Philological Quarterly*, 52 (1973), 119-28.
Atkins, John. *The Art of Ernest Hemingway: His Work and Personality*. London: Spring Books, 1952.
Bader, A. Al. "The Structure of the Modern Short Story." *College English*, 7 (1945), 86-92. Rpt. in May, pp. 107-15.
Baker, Carlos, ed. *Hemingway and His Critics: An International Anthology*. American Century Series. New York: Hill and Wang, 1961.
Barbeau, Clayton C. "The Value of a Wart." In Dickson and Smythe, pp. 51-54.
Bates, H. E. "Hemingway's Short Stories." In *The Modern Short Story*. London: Thomas Nelson, 1942. Rpt. in Baker, pp. 71-79.
Benson, Jackson J. *Hemingway: The Writer's Art of Self-Defense*. Minneapolis: Univ. of Minnesota Press, 1969.
----------. ed. *The Short Stories of Ernest Hemingway: Critical Essays*. Durham, N. C.: Duke Univ. Press, 1975.
Blackmur, R. P. *Language as Gesture: Essays in Poetry*. London: George Allen and Unwin, 1954.
Bridgman, Richard. "Ernest Hemingway." In his *The Colloquial Style in America*. New York: Oxford Univ. Press, 1966, pp. 195-230. Rpt. in Wagner, pp. 160-88.
Brooks, Cleanth, and Robert Penn Warren. *Understanding Fiction*. 2nd ed. New York: Appleton-Century-Crofts, 1959.
Brown, Dennis. "Literature and Existential Psychoanalysis: 'My Kinsman, Major Molineux' and 'Young Goodman Brown.'" *The Canadian Review of American Studies*, 4 (1973), 65-73.
Browning, Preston M., Jr. *Flannery O'Connor*. Crosscurrents Modern Critiques Series. Ed. Harry T. Moore. Carbondale: Southern Illinois Univ. Press, 1974.
Burke, Kenneth. *A Grammar of Motives*. Berkeley: Univ. of California Press, 1969.
----------. *Language as Symbolic Action: Essays on Life, Literature, and Method*. Berkeley: Univ. of California Press, 1966.
Carpenter, Frederick I. *American Literature and the Dream*. New York: The Philosophical Library, 1955.
Coles, Robert. *Flannery O'Connor's South*. Baton Rouge: Louisiana State Univ. Press, 1980.
Connors, Thomas E. "'My Kinsman, Major Molineux': A Reading." *Modern Language Notes*, 74 (1959), 299-302.
Cook, Reginald. "The Forest of Goodman Brown's Night: A Reading of

Hawthorne's 'Young Goodman Brown.'" *The New England Quarterly*, 43 (1970), 473-81.

Crews, Frederick C. *The Sins of the Fathers: Hawthorne's Psychological Themes*. New York: Oxford Univ. Press, 1966.

Daniel, Robert. "Hemingway and His Heroes." *Queen's Quarterly*, 54 (1947), 71-85.

Davis, William V. "'The Fell of Dark': The Loss of Time in Hemingway's 'The Killers.'" *Studies in Short Fiction*, 15 (1978), 319-20.

Dickson, Frank A., and Sandra Smythe, eds. *Handbook of Short Story Writing*. Cincinnati: Writers Digest, 1970.

Diehl, Huston. "Inversion, Parody, and Irony: The Visual Rhetoric of Renaissance English Tragedy." *Studies in English Literature*, 22 (Spring 1982), 197-209.

Driskell, Leon V., and Joan T. Brittain. *The Eternal Crossroads: The Art of Flannery O'Connor*. Lexington: The Univ. Press of Kentucky, 1971.

Dusenbery, Robert. "Hawthorne's Merry Company: The Anatomy of Laughter in the Tales and Short Stories." *PMLA*, 82 (1967), 285-88.

Eggenschwiler, David. *The Christian Humanism of Flannery O'Connor*. Detroit: Wayne State Univ. Press, 1972.

Eliot, T. S. *The Sacred Wood: Essays on Poetry and Criticism*. London: Methuen, 1950.

Elliott, Gary D. "Hemingway's 'Hills Like White Elephants.'" *The Explicator*, 35 (1977), 22-23.

Empson, William. *Seven Types of Ambiguity*. 3rd ed. New York: World Publishing, 1955.

Engelken, Ruth. "Writing with Description." In Dickson and Smythe, pp. 75-80.

Eschholz, Paul A. "Mark Twain and the Language of Gesture." *Mark Twain Journal*, 17 (1973), 5-8.

Feeley, Sister Kathleen. *Flannery O'Connor: Voice of the Peacock*. New Brunswick, N. J.: Rutgers Univ. Press, 1972.

Ficken, Carl. "Point of View in the Nick Adams Stories." In *Fitzgerald/Hemingway Annual*. Ed. Mathew J. Bruccoli and C. E. Frazer Clark, Jr. Washington, D. C.: N.C.R., 1971, pp. 212-35. Rpt. in Benson, pp. 93-112.

Fogle, Richard Harter. *Hawthorne's Fiction: The Light and Dark*. Norman: Univ. of Oklahoma Press, 1964.

Friedman, Melvin J., and Lewis A. Lawson, eds. *The Added Dimensions: The Art and Mind of Flannery O'Connor*. New York: Fordham Univ. Press, 1966.

Friedman, Norman. "What Makes a Short Story Short?" *Modern Fiction Studies*, 4 (1968), 349-54. Rpt. in May, pp. 131-46.

Gable, Sister Mariella. "Ecumenic Core in Flannery O'Connor's Fiction." *The American Benedictine Review*, 15 (1964), 127-43.

Gallagher, Edward J. "The Concluding Paragraph of 'Young Goodman Brown.'" *Studies in Short Fiction*, 12 (1975), 29-30.

Gargano, James W. "The 'Look' as a Major Event in James's Short Fiction." *Arizona Quarterly*, 43 (1979), 303-20.

Garnica, Olga K. "Rules of Verbal Interaction and Literary Analysis." *Poetics*, 6 (1977), 155-68.

Gordimer, Nadine. "The Flash of Fireflies." In May, pp. 178-81.

Gullason, Thomas A. "The Short Story: An Underrated Art." *Studies in Short Fiction*, 2 (1964), 13-31. Rpt. in May, pp. 13-31.

Gurko, Leo. *Ernest Hemingway and the Pursuit of Heroism*. New York: Thomas Y. Crowell, 1968.

Hagemann, Meyly Chin. "Hemingway's Secret: Visual to Verbal Art." *Journal*

of Modern Literature, 7 (1979), 87-112.
Hendin, Josephine. The World of Flannery O'Connor. Bloomington: Indiana Univ. Press, 1970.
Hills, Rust. Writing in General and the Short Story in Particular: An Informal Textbook. Boston: Houghton Mifflin, 1977.
Hilton, James. "Creating a 'Lovable Character.'" In Dickson and Smythe, pp. 55-57.
Hoffman, Daniel E. Form and Fable in American Fiction. New York: Oxford Univ. Press, 1961.
Holder, Alan. "The Other Hemingway." In Twentieth Century Literature, 37 (1963), 153-57. Rpt. in Wagner, pp. 103-09.
James, Henry. "The Art of Fiction." In Partial Portraits. Ann Arbor: The Univ. of Michigan Press, 1970, pp. 375-408.
----------. Hawthorne. London: Macmillan, 1879.
Johnston, Kenneth G. "'Hills Like White Elephants': Lean Vintage Hemingway." Studies in American Fiction, 10 (Autumn 1982), 233-38.
----------. "'The Killers': The Background and the Manuscripts." Studies in Short Fiction, 19 (Summer 1982), 247-51.
Kesterson, David B. "Nature and Theme in 'Young Goodman Brown.'" The Dickinson Review, 2 (1970), 42-45.
Lawrence, D. H. "In Our Time: A Review." In his Phoenix. New York: Viking Press, 1936. Rpt. in Weeks, pp. 93-94.
Lesser, Simon O. "The Image of the Father: A Reading of 'My Kinsman, Major Molineux' and 'I Want to Know Why.'" Partisan Review, 22 (1955), 372-90.
Liebman, Sheldon W. "Robin's Conversion: The Design of 'My Kinsman, Major Molineux.'" Studies in Short Fiction, 8 (1971), 443-57.
Lid, Richard W. "Hemingway and The Need for Speech." Modern Fiction Studies, 8 (1962), 401-07.
Long, Chester Clayton. The Liberal Art of Interpretation. New York: Harper and Row, 1974.
Marcus, Mordecai. "What Is an Initiation Story?" The Journal of Aesthetics and Art Criticism, 14 (1960), 221-27. Rpt. with revisions in May, pp. 189-201.
May, Charles E., ed. Short Story Theories. Athens: Ohio Univ. Press, 1976.
Maynard, Reid. "Leitmotif and Irony in Hemingway's 'Hills Like White Elephants.'" University Review, 37 (1971), 272-75.
McFarland, Dorothy Tuck. Flannery O'Connor. New York: Frederick Ungar Publishing, 1976.
McKeithan, D. M. "Hawthorne's 'Young Goodman Brown': An Interpretation." Modern Language Notes, 67 (1952), 93-96.
Miller, Edwin Haviland. "'My Kinsman, Major Molineux': The Playful Art of Nathaniel Hawthorne." ESQ, 24 (1978), 145-51.
Moloney, Michael F. "Ernest Hemingway: The Missing Third Dimension." In Fifty Years of the American Novel. Ed. Harold C. Gardiner. New York: Charles Scribner's Sons, 1951.
Muller, Gilbert H. Nightmares and Visions: Flannery O'Connor and The Catholic Grotesque. Athens: Univ. of Georgia Press, 1971.
Newman, Franklin B. "'My Kinsman, Major Molineux': An Interpretation." The University of Kansas City Review, 21 (1955), 203-12.
Nitzsche, J. C. "House Symbolism in Hawthorne's 'My Kinsman, Major Molineux.'" The American Transcendental Quarterly, 38 (1978), 167-75.
O'Connor, Frank. The Lonely Voice: A Study of The Short Story. Cleveland: The World Publishing Company, 1963. Rpt. in May, pp. 83-93.
Owen, Charles A., Jr. "Time and The Contagion of Flight in 'The Killers.'" Forum, 3 (1960), 45-46.

Paden, Frances Freeman. "Autistic Gestures in *The Heart Is a Lonely Hunter.*" *Modern Fiction Studies*, 28 (Autumn 1982), 453-63.

Paul, Louis. "A Psychoanalytic Reading of Hawthorne's 'Major Molineux': The Father Manque and the Protege Manque." *American Imago*, 18 (1961), 279-88.

Pearce, Roy Harvey. "Robin Molineux on the Analyst's Couch: A Note on the Limits of Psychoanalytic Criticism." *Criticism*, 1 (1959), 83-90.

Perrine, Lawrence. *Literature: Structure, Sound, and Sense.* New York: Harcourt, Brace, 1970.

Plimpton, George. "An Interview with Ernest Hemingway." *The Paris Review*, 18 (1958), 60-89. Rpt. in Wagner, pp. 21-38.

Portch, Stephen R. "A Good Man Is Hard to Find." *The Explicator*, 37 (1978), 19-20.

Portune, Robert. "Collaborators Anonymous." In Dickson and Smythe, pp. 66-70.

Rabate, Jean-Michel. "Silence in *Dubliners.*" In *James Joyce: New Perspectives*. Ed. Colin McCabe. Brighton: Indiana Univ. Press, 1982, 45-72.

Rodrigues, Eusebio L. "'Hills Like White Elephants': An Analysis." *Literary Criterion*, 5 (1962), 105-09.

Rohrberger, Mary. "Hawthorne's Literary Theory and the Nature of His Short Stories." *Studies in Short Fiction*, 3 (1965), 23-30.

Ross, Lillian. "How Do You Like It Now, Gentlemen?" *New Yorker*, 13 (May 1950). Rpt. in Weeks, pp. 17-39.

Rovit, Earl. *Ernest Hemingway.* Twayne's United States Authors Series. Ed. Sylvia E. Bowman. New York: Twayne Publishers, 1963.

Stephens, Martha. *The Question of Flannery O'Connor.* Baton Rouge: Louisiana State Univ. Press, 1973.

Stone, Edward. "Some Questions About Hemingway's 'The Killers.'" *Studies in Short Fiction*, 5 (1967), 12-17.

Strong, L. A. G. "The Story: Notes at Random." *Lovat Dickson's Magazine*, 2 (1934), 281-82.

Trilling, Lionel. "Commentary on 'Hills Like White Elephants.'" In *The Experience of Literature*. New York: Holt, Rinehart, and Winston, 1967, pp. 729-32.

Wagenknecht, Edward. *Nathaniel Hawthorne: Man and Writer.* New York: Oxford Univ. Press, 1961.

Wagner, Linda Welshimer, ed. *Ernest Hemingway: Five Decades of Criticism.* East Lansing: Michigan State Univ. Press, 1974.

Waldhorn, Arthur. *A Reader's Guide to Ernest Hemingway.* New York: Farrar, Straus and Giroux, 1972.

Wallins, Roger P. "Robin and the Narrator in 'My Kinsman, Major Molineux.'" *Studies in Short Fiction*, 12 (1975), 173-79.

Walters, Dorothy. *Flannery O'Connor.* Twayne United States Authors Series. Ed. Sylvia E. Bowman. Boston: Twayne Publishers, 1973.

Weeks, Robert P., ed. *Hemingway: A Collection of Critical Essays.* The Twentieth Century Views Series. Englewood Cliffs, N. J.: Prentice-Hall, 1962.

Welty, Eudora. "The Reading and Writing of Short Stories." *The Atlantic Monthly*, 183 (February 1949), pp. 46-49 and 54-58. Rpt. in May, pp. 159-77.

Young, Philip. *Ernest Hemingway: A Reconsideration.* University Park: The Pennsylvania State Univ. Press, 1966.

----------. "Focus on *To Have and Have Not*, To Have Not: Tough Luck." *Tough*

164

Guy Writers of The Thirties. Crosscurrents Modern Critiques Series. Ed.
David Madden. Carbondale: Southern Illinois Univ. Press, 1968, pp.
42-50.

Nonverbal Research Sources

Argyle, Michael. *Bodily Communication.* New York: International Universities
Press, 1975.
----------, and Mark Cook. *Gaze and Mutual Gaze.* Cambridge: Cambridge Univ.
Press, 1975.
Burgoon, dJudee K., and Thomas Saine. *The Unspoken Dialogue: An Introduction
to Nonverbal Communication.* Boston: Houghton Mifflin, 1978.
Cortes, Juan B., and Florence M. Gatti. "Physique and Propensity."
Psychology Today, 4 (1970), 42-44 and 82-84.
Critchley, Macdonald. *The Language of Gesture.* London: Folcroft-Edward
Arnold, 1970.
Davitz, Joel R., et al. *The Communication of Emotional Meaning.* New York:
McGraw-Hill, 1964.
Ekman, Paul. "Biological and Cultural Contributions to Body and Facial
Movement." In *The Anthropology of the Body.* Ed. John Blacking. London:
Academic Press, 1977, pp. 39-84.
----------, Wallace Friesen, and John Bear. "The International Language of
Gesture." *Psychology Today,* May 1984, 64-79.
----------, and Wallace Friesen. "Nonverbal Leakage and Clues to Deception."
Psychiatry, 32 (1969), 88-106.
----------, and Wallace Friesen. "The Repertoire of Nonverbal Behavior:
Categories, Origins, Usage and Coding." *Semiotics,* 1 (1969), 49-98.
Elam, Keir. *The Semiotics of Theatre and Drama.* New York: Methuen, 1980.
Goffman, Erving. *Interaction Ritual.* New York: Doubleday, 1967.
Hall, Edward T. *Beyond Culture.* Garden City, N. Y.: Anchor Books, 1976.
----------. *The Hidden Dimension.* Garden City, N. Y.: Anchor Books, 1969.
----------. *The Silent Language.* Garden City, N. Y.: Anchor Books, 1959.
----------, and Mildred Hall. "The Sounds of Silence." *Playboy,* June 1971,
pp. 138-40, 148, 204, 206.
Harris, Christie, and Moira Johnston. *Figleafing Through History: The
Dynamics of Dress.* New York: Atheneum, 1972.
Harrison, Randall P. "Nonverbal Communication." In *Handbook of
Communication.* Ed. Ithiel de Sola Pool, et. al. Chicago: Rand McNally,
1973, pp. 93-115.
Hinde, R. A., ed. *Non-verbal Communication.* Cambridge: Cambridge Univ.
Press, 1972.
Jensen, J. Vernon. "Communicative Functions of Silence." *ETC.: A Review of
General Semantics,* 30 (1973), 249-57.
Key, Mary Ritchie. *Paralanguage and Kinesics.* Metuchen, N. J.: The
Scarecrow Press, 1975.
Meerloo, Joost. *Unobtrusive Communication: Essays in Psycholinguistics.*
Assen, Netherlands: Van Gorcum, 1964.
Mehrabian, Albert. *Nonverbal Communication.* Chicago: Aldine Atherton, 1972.
Miller, Jonathan. "Plays and Players." In Hinde, pp. 359-73.
Montagu, Ashley. *Touching: The Human Significance of the Skin.* New York:
Columbia Univ. Press, 1971.
Obermayer, M. E. *Psychocutaneous Medicine.* Springfield, Il.: Charles C.
Thomas, 1966.

O'Donovan, J. W. *Dermatological Neuroses*. London: Kegan Paul, 1927.
Poyatos, Fernando. *New Perspectives in Nonverbal Communication: Studies in Cultural Anthropology, Social Psychology, Linguistics, Literature, and Semiotics*. Oxford: Pergamon, 1983.
Reimer, Morris D. "The Averted Gaze." *Psychiatric Quarterly*, 23 (1949), 108-15.
Ross, John Robert. "On Declarative Sentences." In *Readings in English Transformational Grammar*. Ed. Roderick A. Jacobs and Peter S. Rosenbaum. Boston: Ginn, 1970, pp. 222-72.
Samarin, William J. "Language of Silence." *Practical Anthropology*, 12 (1965), 115-19.
Sapir, Edward. "The Unconscious Patterning of Behavior in Society." In *The Unconscious: A Symposium*. Ed. E. S. Drummer. New York: Alfred A. Knopf, 1927, pp. 114-42. Rpt. in *Selected Writings of Edward Sapir in Language, Culture, and Personality*. Ed. David E. Mandelbaum. Berkeley: Univ. of California Press, 1949.
Van Hooff, J. A. R. A. M. "A Comparative Approach to the Phylogeny of Laughter and Smiling." In Hinde, pp. 209-41.

Works Consulted

Barker, Larry L. and Nancy B. Collins. "Nonverbal and Kinesic Research." In *Methods of Research in Communication*. Ed. P. Emmert and W. D. Brooks. Boston: Houghton Mifflin, 1970, pp. 343-71.
Bates, H. E. "The Modern Short Story: Retrospect." In *The Modern Short Story: A Critical Survey*. 1941; rpt. Boston: The Writer, 1972. Rpt. in May, pp. 72-79.
Berscheid, Ellen, Elaine Walster, and George Bohrnstedt. "Body Image: The Happy American Body." *Psychology Today*, 7 (1973), 119-23 and 126-31.
Burke, Kenneth. *The Philosophy of Literary Form: Studies in Symbolic Action*. 2nd ed. Baton Rouge: Louisiana State Univ. Press, 1967.
Compton, Norma H. "Personal Attributes of Color and Design Preferences in Clothing Fabrics." *Journal of Psychology*, 54 (1962), 191-95.
Cowley, Malcolm. *The Portable Hemingway*. New York: The Viking Press, 1945.
Davis, Flora. *Inside Tuition: What We Know About Nonverbal Communication*. New York: McGraw-Hill, 1973.
Davitz, Joel R., and Lois J. Davitz. "The Communication of Feelings by Content-Free Speech." *Journal of Communication*, 9 (1959), 6-13.
Eisenberg, Abnem, and Ralph R. Smith, Jr. *Nonverbal Communication*. New York: Bobbs-Merrill, 1971.
Ekman, Paul. "Facial Signs: Facts, Fantasies, and Possibilities," In *Sight, Sound, and Sense*. Ed. Thomas A. Sebeck. Bloomington: Indiana Univ. Press, 1978, pp. 124-56.
----------, and Wallace V. Friesen. *The Facial Action Coding System: A Manual for the Measurement of Facial Movement*. Palo Alto, Ca.: Consulting Psychologists' Press, 1977.
----------. "Hand Movements." *The Journal of Communication*, 22 (1972), 353-74.
----------. "Measuring Facial Movement." *Environmental Psychology and Nonverbal Behavior*, 1 (1976), 56-75.
Fabun, Don. *Communications: The Transfer of Meaning*. 2nd ed. Beverly Hills, Ca.: Glencoe Press, 1968.
Fick, Leonard J. *The Light Beyond: A Study of Hawthorne's Theology*.

Westminster, Md.: Newman Press, 1955.

Freud, Sigmund. "Fragment of an Analysis of a Case of Hysteria (1905)." In *Collected Papers*. Vol. III. New York: Basic Books, 1959.

Gibson, James J. "Observations on Active Touch." *Psychological Review*, 69 (1962), 477-91.

Gross, Seymour L. "Hawthorne's 'My Kinsman, Major Molineux': History As Moral Adventure." *Nineteenth Century Fiction*, 12 (1957), 97-109.

Gurel, Lois M., June C. Wilbur, and Lee Gurel. "Personality Correlates of Adolescent Clothing Styles." *Journal of Home Economics*, 64 (1972), 42-47.

Harper, Robert G., Arthur N. Wiens, and Joseph D. Matarazzo. *Nonverbal Communication: The State of the Art*. New York: John Wiley and Sons, 1978.

Harrison, Randall P., and Wayne W. Crouch. "Nonverbal Communication: Theory and Research." In *Communication and Behavior*. Ed. Gerhard J. Hanneman and William J. McEwen. Reading, Ma.: Addison-Wesley, 1975, pp. 76-96.

Jourard, Sidney M. and Paul F. Second. "Body-Cathexis and Personality." *British Journal of Psychology*, 46 (1955), 130-38.

Kostelanetz, Richard. "Notes on the American Short Story Today." *Minnesota Review*, 5 (1966), 214-21. Rpt. in May, pp. 214-25.

Lawrence, D. H. *Studies in Classic American Literature*. 1923; rpt. New York: Doubleday, 1951.

Leavis, Q. D. "Hawthorne as Poet." *Sewanee Review*, 59 (1951), 198-205.

Lesser, Simon O. *Fiction and the Unconscious*. Boston: Beacon Press, 1957.

Lewis, R. W. B. *The American Adam: Innocence, Tragedy, and Tradition in the Nineteenth Century*. Chicago: Univ. of Chicago Press, 1955.

Levy, Phyllis Kempner. "The Ability to Express and Perceive Vocal Communications of Feeling." In *The Communication of Emotional Meaning*. Ed. Joel R. Davitz et al. New York: McGraw-Hill, 1964, pp. 43-55.

Montagu, Ashley. "Communication, Evolution, and Education." In *The Human Dialogue: Perspectives on Communication*. Ed. Floyd W. Matson and Ashley Montagu. New York: Free Press, 1967, pp. 445-55.

O'Connor, Flannery. *The Complete Stories*. New York: Farrar, Straus and Giroux, 1971.

Paulits, Walter J. "Ambivalence in 'Young Goodman Brown.'" *American Literature*, 41 (1970), 577-84.

Ruesch, Jurgen, and Weldon Kees. "Function and Meaning in the Physical Environment." In *Environmental Psychology*. Ed. H. M. Proshansky, W. H. Ittelson, and L. G. Rivlin. New York: Holt, Rinehart, and Winston, 1969, pp. 141-53.

Schloss, Carol. *Flannery O'Connor's Dark Comedies*. Southern Literary Studies Series. Ed. Louis D. Rubin, Jr. Baton Rouge: Louisiana State Univ. Press, 1980.

Smith, Howard A. "Nonverbal Communication in Teaching." *Review of Educational Research*, 49 (1979), 631-72.

Trollope, Anthony. "The Genius of Nathaniel Hawthorne." *North American Review*, 129 (1879), 203-22.

Van Doren, Mark. *Nathaniel Hawthorne*. New York: W. Sloane, 1949.

Waggoner, Hyatt H. *Hawthorne: A Critical Study*. Cambridge, Ma.: The Belknap Press of Harvard Univ. Press, 1963.

INDEX

Coles, Robert 144n
Connors, Thomas E. 57, 86n
Cook, Mark 80, 87n, 128, 146n
Cook, Reginald 87n
Copard, A. E. 39
Cortes, J. B. 145n
Crane, Stephen 6, 10, 25n
Crews, Frederick C. 32, 49, 80, 85n, 87n
Critchley, MacDonald 34, 43n
Cultural Distinctions 2-3, 9, 16, 20, 153, 155-156

Daniel, Robert 112, 113n, 114n, 116n
Davitz, Joel 147, 157n
Davis, William V. 113n
"Defender Of The Faith" 12, 26n
Dickens, Charles 38, 154
Diehl, Huston 33, 43n
Disorientation 55, 69, 83, 84, 92, 113n, 150
Drama 4, 7, 32-36, 153
    Eastern 32
    Renaissance 33
Dramatic Monologue 31
Driskell, Leon V. 144n
"Dubliners" 41, 45n
Dusenbery, Robert 50, 52, 76, 85n, 87n

East Of Eden 22, 27
Eggenschwiler, David 120, 144n, 145n
Einstein, Albert 147
Ekman, Paul 2, 5, 7, 8, 9, 10, 11, 16, 22, 24, 25n, 26n, 29, 39
Elam, Keir 43n
Eliot, T. S. 3, 4, 25n, 111
Elliott, Gary D. 107, 115n
Emblems 8, 9, 11
Emotions 2, 3, 4, 9, 10, 17, 76, 80, 90, 95, 98, 109, 112, 122, 147, 156
Empson, William 150, 157n
Endings 49, 75, 84, 109, 120, 138, 143
Engelken, Ruth 44n
Environment 2, 22, 30, 61, 64, 69, 78, 83, 87n, 97, 99, 102, 132, 138-139, 151, 155
Eschholz, Paul A. 34, 35, 36, 37, 43n
Eyes 1, 4, 6, 12, 13, 15, 19
    in Hawthorne 55, 58, 59, 63, 69, 71, 72, 74, 79, 82
    in Hemingway 96, 98, 99
    in O'Connor 121-122, 125-129, 131-134, 136

Faulkner, William 154
Features 13, 15, 71, 82, 95, 124-125, 127, 133
Feeley, Kathleen 119, 136, 145n, 146n
Fogle, Richard Harter 49, 52, 75, 77, 78, 81, 84, 85n, 86n, 87n, 88n
"For Esme -- With Love And Squalor" 5, 25n
Ficken, Carl 93, 114n
Friedman, Melvin J. 118, 119, 144n, 145n
Friedman, Norman 37, 44n

DATE DUE